In Quest
of God

SWAMI RAMDAS
1884 - 1963

In Quest of God

The Saga of an Extraordinary Pilgrimage

SWAMI RAMDAS

FOREWORD BY
RAM DASS (RICHARD ALPERT)

PREFACE BY
EKNATH EASWARAN

BLUE DOVE PRESS
SAN DIEGO, CALIFORNIA • 1994

Also available from Blue Dove Press by Swami Ramdas—
In the Vision of God – volumes I & II

Blue Dove Press publishes books by and about saints of all religions as well as other inspiring works. It also distributes similar books by other publishers as well as a newsletter, "The Blue Dove." Catalog sent free upon request. Blue Dove also offers a catalog of other works by Swami Ramdas. Write to:

BLUE DOVE PRESS
Post Office Box 261611
San Diego, CA 92196
Phone: (800) 691-1008
FAX: (619) 271-5695

Copyright © 1994 by Anandashram Trust
All rights reserved
Printed in the United States. First American edition

Cover and text design:
Brian Moucka, Poppy Graphics, Santa Barbara, Cal.

Special thanks to Dr. Lance Nelson,
University of San Diego, for inspired and unstinting help.

ISBN: 1-884997-01-5

Library of Congress Cataloging in Publication data:

Ramdas, Swami, 1884-1963.
    In Quest of God: the saga of an extraordinary pilgrimage / by Swami Ramdas; foreword by Ram Dass (Richard Alpert); preface by Eknath Easwaran.
        p. cm.
        ISBN 1-884997-00-7 (Hardbound). -- ISBN 1-884997-01-5 (Soft bound)
        1. Ramdas, Swami, 1884-1963. 2. Hindus--India--Biography.
    I. Title.
    B11175.R346A3 1994
    294.5'092--dc20
        [B]   94-12042
                                                                    CIP

Life can be understood only by going to the very root of it. And the root is ever sweet and eternal.

—Swami Ramdas

To those who always remain absorbed in remembrance of Me, to those always harmonious, they are ever in My care.

—Bhagavad Gita 9:22

The path of Swami Ramdas' pilgrimage as chronicled in this book.

Contents

Foreword by Ram Dass (Richard Alpert)	xi
Preface by Sri Eknath Easwaran	xiii
Introduction by Swami Satchidananda	xxi
Author's Preface	1
1. Struggle and Initiation	3
2. Renunciation	5
3. Adoption of Sannyas	7
4. Srirangam	9
5. Rameshwaram	13
6. Madura	15
7. Chidambaram	17
8. Journey to Tirupapuliyur	21
9. Pondicherry and Tiruvannamalai	23
10. In the Cave	27
11. Tirupati	29
12. God is Everywhere	33
13. A Kind Policeman	35
14. Jagannath Puri	39
15. Christ, a Messenger of God	41
16. Calcutta and Dakshineshwar	45
17. Taraknath Temple	51
18. Kashi	55

19. LOVE CONQUERS HATE	59
20. JHANSI	61
21. MEDITATION: THE ONLY WAY	65
22. RAM, THE FRIEND OF THE POOR	67
23. GOD NEVER PUNISHES	69
24. HIMALAYAN JOURNEY	75
25. HIMALAYAN JOURNEY (CONTINUED)	79
26. HIMALAYAN JOURNEY (CONTINUED)	83
27. MATHURA, GOKUL AND BRINDABAN	87
28. RAIPUR	91
29. AJMERE	95
30. MONEY IS THE ROOT OF ALL EVIL	99
31. JUNAGAD	101
32. MUCHKUND RISHI'S ASHRAM AND DWARAKA	107
33. BOMBAY	111
34. PANCHAVATI AND TAPOVAN	117
35. TRIMBAKESHWAR	121
36. PANDHARPUR–BIJAPUR	125
37. SRI SIDDHARUDHA SWAMI	131

APPENDIX

IN THE CAVE	137
POEMS	153
LETTERS	155
GLOSSARY	161

Foreword by Ram Dass (Richard Alpert)

In 1967, I met my guru, Neem Karoli Baba. After the initial shock of meeting such a being, I became aware that his thumb was continually moving up and down the fingers of his hand, stopping momentarily at each joint. When I questioned his Indian devotees, I was told that he was continuously doing Ram mantra, the repetition of one of the names of God, his fingers serving like the beads of a *mala* (rosary).

Later, in 1973, after he left his body, I was told that he kept a 'diary.' I was most curious as to what such an enlightened being would find worthy of committing to paper. When I was finally shown the exercise books which served as his diary, I found page after page, book after book, in his Hindi script, of the name RAM, repeated again and again.

From the first time I started to work with beads and the repetition of either the mantra in praise of RAM, "Sri Ram Jai Ram, Jai Jai Ram," or just the single word, "Ram" in 1968, I recognized the potential power of this simple devotional technique to rend the veil of ignorance from moment to moment thus allowing one to imbue one's life with spirit.

It was easy to keep the mantra going in my room in the ashram, but as I ventured forth into the world, I found that the fascinations, seductions and slings and arrows of daily life so often distracted me from 'remembering.' It was hard for me to imagine how it could be otherwise.

Them in 1970 I came upon the writings of Swami Ramdas

(or 'Papa Ramdas', as I thought of him). And there it was, so innocently presented, a testament to the possibility that by remembering Ram (God), one's life could be transformed, totally transformed, moment by moment, into divine *lila* (play). His very colorful descriptions allowed me to empathetically experience this devotional method from inside.

Swami Ramdas' depth of devotional evolution is far beyond my own, so I appreciate him as true Satsang, a member of the community of spiritual beings who are further along the path, encouraging me onward towards the joy of freedom. I hope that as you join Swami Ramdas through these writings, you will be served in a similar way.

PREFACE BY SRI EKNATH EASWARAN

SWAMI RAMDAS is one of the most lovable and most appealing saints to be found anywhere. He is also one of the most profound, expressing dizzying heights of experience in language as simple and guileless as a child's. And, finally, he is one of the most practical. Everything he tells us is stamped with personal experience—and that makes this little book one of the most remarkable testimonies in the annals of world mysticism.

It was in 1963, only a few months before he shed his body, that my wife and I had the blessing of meeting Swami Ramdas in his ashram or spiritual community in South India. The place is called Anandashram, the abode of joy, and the name fits perfectly. Everything associated with Swami Ramdas seems to radiate joy.

Christine and I arrived a little before noon and were shown into a room where a lot of people had already gathered—eastern and western, men and women and children, some educated and affluent, others uneducated and poor—who had come just to be in his presence. But the object of all this attention—"Papa," as he was known in the ashram—was as unaffected by it as a child. He was seated in a comfortable chair with his radio on, looking just like anybody, listening to the news with a number of people seated around him on the floor. We were introduced to Papa and his beautiful spiritual companion, Mother Krishnabai, his foremost disciple, who later became head of the ashram and continued Ramdas' work. They greeted us very affectionately, as if we had always been part of their ashram family.

So far as I remember, there was not much talk that afternoon. None of us had come to ask questions. We had come simply to absorb the peace and joy that radiates from one who is full of the awareness of God. In India this is called darshan, but it is customary in every religious tradition—or at least was customary until the industrial revolution. A sage or saint may talk a little to satisfy the needs of ordinary communication, but there is no need for them to use words. We simply look at them and draw inspiration from them; and afterwards, perhaps even without our knowledge, we are changed to some extent by that encounter. Even so secular an observer as Somerset Maugham perceived this after his visit to another great sage of South India, Sri Ramana Maharshi.

The very presence of Papa Ramdas comforted and strengthened us. He was visible proof that a man apparently like you and me—not an austere, emaciated monk, but a former textile technician who had lived in the midst of worldly activity—had become established in the awareness of God. Later, when I returned to this country, I used to tell my students, "If a textile technician can become established in the awareness of God, I don't see any reason why the rest of us should feel handicapped because we are chemical engineers or computer programmers or schoolteachers or students." It doesn't make any difference to the Lord at all. He is not going to ask us, "What occupation did you follow?" All that He is going to ask is, "Do you love Me with all your heart, all your mind, all your spirit, and all your strength?"

All of us in his presence that afternoon were invited to stay for the midday meal. That is the ashram tradition. Supplies were brought by wealthy people, not as a favor but as an offering to the Lord, and the cooking was all done by wealthy women who had volunteered their services. The men were helping with the work of the ashram outside. This was their idea of a vacation, and I felt very pleased that this ancient ideal has not been lost.

Ramdas had travelled all over India, and he had maharajas and millionaires as friends as well as the poorest of villagers. He made no distinction among them. All he was interested in was whether the person was sincere in seeking God. And sincere seekers in India are not impressed by media publicity or wealth or a charismatic personality. They look for purity of character, and watch to see how much a person says accords with how he lives. They look for the simplicity, unpretentiousness and humility that mark a great saint's intuitive capacity to live in complete harmony with all of life.

Swami Ramdas not only had these qualities, but two other precious gifts which you will find over and over in these pages: he had a wonderful sense of humor and he loved to tell a story. He must have recounted the adventures in this book countless times to those around him, and I think nobody enjoyed them more than he. After saying something ineffable he will suddenly laugh like a child and add, "That reminds Ramdas of a rather funny incident." (He always spoke of himself in the third person like this, he was so detached even from his own self.) And then he would repeat some unlikely misadventure that had befallen him in the early days of his wandering, recollected as if it were a skit in a high school play. Or, after explaining the stages of God–realization while your intellect reels, he would add, "Today I am just God's child. When I was born, I didn't have a single tooth. Now, as you can see, I don't have any either, so I have become a baby again." And he would laugh with that toothless smile, which reminded me so much of Mahatma Gandhi's.

The Ramdas you will meet in this book is very much like this, yet very different too. The man who relates *In Quest of God* is just beginning his spiritual journey. On the very first page of his prologue he tells us that a kind of bomb has burst in his consciousness, and every page thereafter flares with fire; in the Ramdas I met, all that fire had long since been transmuted into light. *In Quest of God* is thus one of that most precious of human records: a description of the greatest upheaval that can take place in consciousness, the awakening to the call of the spirit within.

Ramdas was in Mangalore at that time and he was not Ramdas, the "servant of God," but Vittal Rao. As so often happens, his awakening came at what Dante calls "the midpoint of man's life," and there had been no hint of anything like it in any of his previous years. Suddenly there is this explosion in his consciousness—something like what happened to the would-be troubadour of Assisi—and everything he has been doing becomes meaningless. The pursuit of money and pleasure and prestige and power, which everyone values, becomes like ashes. Nothing matters to him but that he find God—not somewhere outside him, but in the depths of his own consciousness.

Listen to what he himself tells us of this search: "The river of life struggles through all obstacles and conditions to reach the vast and infinite ocean of existence who is God. It knows no rest, no freedom and no peace until it mingles with the waters of immortality and delights in the visions of infinity." That is pure Ramdas, and every word is stamped with his personal experience. He is telling us how he felt, with what passion he sought; yet he is also telling us about ourselves, about every one of us, and about the whole evolution of the human spirit as it struggles to be reunited with God.

Ramdas travelled all over India, climbed the Himalayas, ceaselessly repeating the *mantram* which had been given to him: *Om Sri Ram, Jai Ram Jai Jai Ram.* This mantram (or mantra, as it is often called) is built around the name of Rama, who is worshipped in India as an incarnation of God, and whose name comes from a Sanskrit root meaning "joy." *Rama* means "the source of abiding joy," and either by itself or in combination with other words, as in Ramdas' phrase, it is one of the most ancient and most popular mantrams in India. Today, I believe, it must be known all over the world, because

Rama is the mantram used by Mahatma Gandhi. But it is important to understand that *Rama* here does not refer to an exotic Hindu deity; it is simply a name for God. In another marvelous book, *The Way of a Pilgrim*, we find an anonymous Russian seeker setting out just like Ramdas, leaving all behind him as Jesus enjoins in the Gospels, and ceaselessly repeating in his heart the Orthodox mantram, the Jesus Prayer. It is exactly the same thing; only the languages differ.

After his pilgrimages were over, Ramdas returned to his native place, on the Southwestern coast of India. He came back to share the joy of God with everybody. That is what happens. You can't keep it to yourself, because there is no separate you any longer. Ramdas was full to overflowing with this joy, this unshakable security, this love and wisdom, and the rest of his time on earth was spent in giving it freely to all who came to him.

I compared Ramdas' story with *The Way of a Pilgrim* to emphasize what is the same in both East and West. But there is also an important difference. Throughout the West, this way of taking to the spiritual life has all but disappeared, and even in medieval times these reckless souls who abandoned every worldly thing to search for God on a pilgrim's endless road were rare. In India, by contrast, this has been part of our religion for thousands of years, as far back as any records reach. When Ramdas left job and family and name behind him, he was not "dropping out" of society as such an act would amount to in the West. He simply chose another order of society, joining a living stream of *sadhus* or seekers who have had a place in our ancient culture since time began. Despite all its immense difficulties (you will read about them in this book), it is a life that has its own support within our civilization.

That is why, whenever I recommend Swami Ramdas in the West, I always say, "Draw inspiration from him, but do not try to imitate him literally." Do not abandon your partner in Des Moines and start out on foot for the nearest holy place without so much as a quarter to your name. Holy places in this country are not easily found, and unless you have the stature of a Saint Francis or Saint Teresa, the dangers of this way of life today are so immense that they are much more likely to impede your spiritual progress than to aid it.

If you feel inspired to follow Swami Ramdas' example, what I would recommend is just as challenging and rewarding. Follow the spirit of what he has done. You do not have to give up your family and your job and travel to exotic places to find God. He—or She—is as near as your heart. The only barrier is our selfishness, our personal passions and attachments, the fierce sense of *I* and *me* and *mine* that makes us pursue what we want even at the cost of those around us. It is a tremendous challenge, but we can learn to dissolve these self-centered attachments right in the midst of family and friends, working at a job that contributes to society in some measure. And we can do it just the way Ramdas did: through repetition of a mantram or Holy Name.

In fact, the greatest inspiration this precious book offers is the power of the mantram, which is open to all. You don't have to be a Hindu to use a mantram. Every religion has a mantram, often more than one, hallowed for centuries by devoted repetition of sincere seekers and saints. For Christians, the very name of Jesus by itself is one of the oldest mantrams, and the Jesus Prayer—"Lord, Jesus Christ, have mercy on me"—is used in Orthodox circles very much the way Ramdas repeated the name of *Rama*. (In South India, where the Christian communities trace their traditions back to Thomas the Apostle, the sacred sound *Om* may even be added—*Om Yesu Christu*—very much as in the mantram that Ramdas received from his father.) Catholics may use "Hail Mary" or "Ave Maria." Jews may repeat *Barukh attah Adonai* or the formula hallowed by the Hasidim: *Ribono shel olam*, "Lord of the Universe." Muslims repeat the name of Allah or Allahu akbar, "God is great." And Buddhists repeat *Om mani padme hum*: "*Om!* the jewel in the lotus of the heart," which is divine.

So there is a mantram for every religious background. But,

interestingly enough, the mantram is effective even for a devout atheist or agnostic, as well as for the many people who feel estranged from the religion they were born into because of unpleasant childhood associations. For such people I suggest that they choose any of these traditional mantrams that appeals to them deeply. The Buddhist mantram is popular because it makes no reference to God at all. And if none of these formulas appeals more than any other, I always recommend repeating simply *Rama, Rama, Rama*. It is short, simple, rhythmic, and hallowed by thousands of years of use; and everyone, I think, responds to calling on the source of joy within the heart. Many people feel drawn to it because it was Mahatma Gandhi's mantram, on his lips even when the assassin's bullet found his heart. Finally, if you do get caught in Ramdas' story, I suspect that the name of Ram is very likely to acquire a special appeal of its own.

I have written a whole book about the mantram, so I will resist the temptation to add my words to those of Ramdas about what it can do. But I do ask you to remember, as you read his adventures, that this example can be followed with great artistry right in the midst of the jungles and deserts of modern city life. It will bring an ever-increasing joy not only to you, but to the lives of those around you. Try the mantram for yourself as you read this book—it is so simple to use!—and you will find Ramdas' words unfolding with new meaning as you follow in the spirit of his "quest of God."

Introduction by Swami Satchidananda

The writer is one of the senior disciples of Swami Ramdas. He served Swami Ramdas and Mother Krishnabai (his foremost disciple) for forty years, during which he accompanied them on tours within and outside India. He now manages Anandashram, Kerala, India.

OM SRI RAM JAI RAM JAI JAI RAM

Swami Ramdas, whom his devotees and followers lovingly called Beloved Papa, after attaining the fullest realization of God in all His aspects and the consequent opening of the floodgates of joy in his heart, founded Anandashram near Kanhangad, North Kerala, India in 1931. He was frequently travelling in many parts of India to propagate the glory of the Name of God and dwelt upon his own life as an example of what God's Name could do to a humble person. He had by then written many books. All his writings extol the greatness and glory of the Name, the value of surrender to God's will and also describe what the final spiritual attainment is. His books embodying the essence of his teachings are in good demand the world over.

In 1954 he went on a tour round the world, in the course of which he spent five weeks in USA. He visited New York, St. Paul, Seattle, San Francisco, Carmel and Los Angeles and met many seekers of Truth. He gave talks in various centers, churches, Rotary Clubs, etc. While in New York, one of the friends, Dr. Alexander Imich, who came to see him, discussed various matters, including the need to publish Papa's books in America. Nothing however materialized for years but all the same, the seed that had been sown remained intact. Papa had also desired that his books be published in the USA. Now, after nearly four decades, the seed is sprouting, and our friend Sevakram (Jeff Blom) is prompted from within to make himself responsible for printing and publishing *In Quest of God* and *In The Vision of God* in America through the Blue Dove Press, and to fulfil Papa's long-cherished desire. We wish his noble venture all success. It is decided that after the reprint of these books, Blue Dove Press will also take up other books of Anandashram.

The book *In Quest of God* is written in a simple, beautiful manner. It reads as if the writer has written about another person's spiritual odyssey, as he has used the third person pronoun "Ramdas" instead of the usual first person "I." After a particular stage, he said he could not use "I," and from then on he started talking or writing about himself as "Ramdas."

This book describes his itinerant life as a mendicant *sadhu* after he renounced his hearth and home in 1922 until he reached and stayed at a cave in a place called Mangalore exactly a year later. He was chanting God's name constantly and looked upon the world as the manifestation of RAM (God) and accepted everything that happened as willed by God. This kept him ever bathed in bliss through thick and thin. For an onlooker he appeared like a beggar, a single cloth covering his nakedness, with no place to lay his head on and not sure if he would get his next meal. What was the secret of his ineffable happiness? It was his constant, intimate communion with God, the source of his being. Wealthy persons wondered how he could be so steeped in joy in such an abject condition. His life proved that happiness does not depend upon external conditions. One is eternally happy if one's mind is lost in God-thought whatever may be his external appearance and condition.

The book *In the Vision of God* is a continuation of *In Quest of God* and describes his travels as a child of God all over India many times and how he was taken care of by God tenderly.

After Papa's visit to the USA, he wrote the book *World is God* giving his impressions of the world tour. In this book he refers to his spiritual state thus, "God has made Ramdas into a ripe fruit on His huge tree of manifest life for presentation to the world as a gift. Under His guidance, care and grace, Ramdas' life grew, budded, bloomed and fruitioned until at last it became ripe, sweet and fragrant. Surely all the glory for the production of such a fruit is His—Ramdas' beloved Master's."

Beloved Papa's teachings, stemming from his realized divineness have spread all over India and many parts of Europe, America and other countries judged by the steady flow of visitors to the Ashram all round the year. It is as it should be. *Sadgurus* of Papa's spiritual stature are not many now. In His infinite compassion and love, Papa while in flesh and blood shared readily the fruits of his *tapasya* [austerities] with those prepared to realize God and live, move and have their being in God. Papa did not want them to let the rare opportunity they had to attain spiritual perfection slip. He extended his hand of help to all who hungered for God-realization. When I met him forty-five years ago, I could not help surrendering myself at his feet and looking up to him as a savior. He had the unmistakable stamp of divinity on his face. In his august presence one's ego-sense disappeared for the moment and one sat before Papa like a child gazing at his face with mouth agape. One in wonder exclaimed, 'Is he a second Buddha come to redeem the struggling souls?' Such was the power he exercised over one's mind and soul.

We are sure our American brothers and sisters will welcome this publication of Papa's books in the USA, which will ensure easy availability of the books for the earnest seekers and others interested in the things of the spirit.

Jai Sadgurudev

To the Reader

This book is a complete and unabridged edition of Swami Ramdas' work. Spelling, punctuation and capitalization have been changed to conform to American usage but the text is otherwise word for word as originally written.

In most cases the first time Indian words appear there is a definition in a footnote. In addition there is a complete glossary at the end of the book that sometimes has a more complete definition than appears in the footnote. Indian words are in italics, with the exception of the word "sadhu" (wandering monk), which appears numerous times.

Swami Ramdas expressed himself only in the third person, as reflected in this work.

In Quest of God is the first book of a trilogy describing Swami Ramdas' spiritual pilgrimage. The next two parts (*In the Vision of God* volumes I & II) are also published by Blue Dove Press.

O RAM, THE TRUTH—THE LOVE—THE GOAL OF HUMAN PERFECTION—ALL HAIL—ALL HAIL!

It was about two years[1] ago that Ram first kindled in the heart of His humble slave, Ramdas, a keen desire to realize His Infinite Love. To strive to approach and understand Ram is to recede from the world of vanishing forms, because Ram is the only Truth—the only Reality. Ram is a subtle and mysterious power that pervades and sustains the whole universe. Birthless and deathless is He. He is present in all things and in all creatures, who only appear as separate entities due to their ever-changing forms. To wake up from this illusion of forms is to realize at once the Unity or Love of Ram. Love of Ram means Love of all beings, all creatures, all things in this world, because Ram is in all and all is in Ram, and Ram is all in all. To realize this Great Truth we who, through ignorance, feel as separate individuals, should submit ourselves to the will and working of that Infinite power—that Infinite Love—Ram, who is one and all-pervading. By a complete surrender to the will of Ram, we lose consciousness of the body which keeps us aloof from Him, and find ourselves in a state of complete identification and union with Ram, who is in us and everywhere around us. In this condition, hatred, which means consciousness of diversity, ceases, and Love, consciousness of Unity, is realized. This Divine Love can be attained by humbling ourselves to such a degree as to totally subdue our egoism, our self-assertion as a separate individual existence. Having reached this stage, we, by the awakened consciousness of Unity or Love,

---
[1] In 1920

are naturally prompted to sacrifice all the interests that concern the body, for the welfare of our fellowmen and fellow-creatures, who are all manifestations of the same Ram. This was the great sacrifice of Buddha, of Jesus Christ and has been of Mahatma Gandhi in our own times. These three great men are the fullest manifestations of Ram—the Great Truth—the Infinite Love. *Om Sri Ram!*

1.

STRUGGLE AND INITIATION

FOR NEARLY A YEAR, Ramdas struggled on in a world full of cares, anxieties and pains. It was a period of terrible stress and restlessness—all of his own making. In this utterly helpless condition, full of misery, "Where is relief? Where is rest?" was the heart's cry of Ramdas. The cry was heard, and from the Great Void came the voice, "Despair not! Trust Me and thou shalt be free!"—and this was the voice of Ram. These encouraging words of Ram proved like a plank thrown towards a man struggling for very life in the stormy waves of a raging sea. The great assurance soothed the aching heart of helpless Ramdas, like gentle rain on thirsting earth. Thenceforward, a part of the time that was formerly totally devoted to worldly affairs was taken up for the meditation of Ram who, for that period, gave him real peace and relief. Gradually love for Ram—the Giver of peace—increased. The more Ramdas meditated on and uttered His name, the greater the relief and joy he felt. Nights, which are free from worldly duties were, in course of time, utilized for *Ram-bhajan*[1] with scarcely one or two hours rest. His devotion for Ram progressed by leaps and bounds.

During the day, when cares and anxieties were besetting him due to monetary and other troubles, Ram was coming to his aid in unexpected ways. So, whenever free from worldly

---

[1] *Ram-bhajan:* devotional singing

duties—be the period ever so small—he would meditate on Ram and utter His name. Walking in the streets he would be uttering, "Ram, Ram." Ramdas was now losing attraction for the objects of the world. Sleep, except for one or two hours in the night, was given up for the sake of Ram. Fineries in clothes and dress were replaced by coarse *khaddar*[2] Bed was substituted by a bare mat. Food, first two meals were reduced to one meal a day and after some time this too was given up for plantains[3] and boiled potatoes. Chilies and salt were totally eschewed. No taste but for Ram. Meditation of Ram continued apace. It encroached upon the hours of the day and the so-called worldly duties.

At this stage one day, Ramdas' father came to him, sent by Ram, and calling him aside, gave him the *upadesh*[4] of *Ram-mantram*—"Sri Ram, Jai Ram, Jai Jai Ram," assuring him that if he repeated this *mantram* at all times, Ram would give him eternal happiness. This initiation from the father—who has thereafter been looked upon by Ramdas as *Gurudev*—hastened on the aspirant in his spiritual progress. Off and on he was prompted by Ram to read the teachings of Sri Krishna—The *Bhagavad Gita*, Buddha—*Light of Asia*, Jesus Christ—"New Testament," Mahatma Gandhi—*Young India* and *Ethical Religion*. The young plant of *bhakti*[5] in Ram was thus nurtured in the electric atmosphere created by the influence of these great men on the mind of humble Ramdas. It was at this time that it slowly dawned upon his mind that Ram was the only Reality and all else was false. Whilst desires for the enjoyment of worldly things were fast falling off, the consideration of *me* and *mine* was also wearing out. The sense of possession and relationship was vanishing. All thought, all mind, all heart, all soul was concentrated on Ram, Ram covering up and absorbing everything.

---

[2] *Khaddar*: home spun cloth
[3] *plantain*: a kind of large banana
[4] *upadesh*: initiation
[5] *bhakti*: devotion to God

2.

RENUNCIATION

NOW FROM THE narrow pond of a worldly life, Ram had lifted up his slave to throw him into the extensive ocean of a Universal Life. But to swim in the wide ocean, Ram knew, Ramdas wanted strength and courage, for gaining which Ram intended to make his ignorant and untrained slave to pass through a course of severe discipline, and this under His direct guidance and support. So one night while engaged in drinking in the sweetness of His name, Ramdas was made to think in the following strain:

O Ram, when Thy slave finds Thee at once so powerful and so loving, and that he who trusts Thee can be sure of true peace and happiness, why should he not throw himself entirely on Thy mercy, which can only be possible by giving up everything he called "mine"? Thou art all in all to Thy slave. Thou art the sole Protector in the world. Men are deluded when they declare, "I do this, I do that. This is mine, that is mine." All, O Ram, is Thine, and all things are done by Thee alone. Thy slave's one prayer to Thee is to take him under Thy complete guidance and remove his "I"-ness.

This prayer was heard. Ramdas' heart heaved a deep sigh. A hazy desire to renounce all and wander over the earth in the garb of a mendicant—in quest of Ram—wafted over his mind. Now Ram prompted him to open at random the book, *Light of Asia* which was before him at the time. His eyes rested upon the pages wherein is described the great renunciation of Buddha, who says:

> For now the hour is come when I should quit
> This golden prison, where my heart lives caged,
> To find the Truth; which henceforth I will seek,
> For all men's sake, until the truth be found.

Then Ramdas similarly opened the New Testament and lighted upon the following definite words of Jesus Christ:

> And everyone that hath forsaken houses or brethren or sisters, or father or mother or wife or children or lands for my name's sake, shall receive a hundredfold and shall inherit everlasting life.

Then again he was actuated in the same way to refer to the *Bhagavad Gita*—and he read the following *sloka*[1]:

> Abandoning all duties, come to Me alone for shelter, sorrow not. I will liberate thee from all sins.

Ram had thus spoken out through the words of these three great *avatars*[2]—Buddha, Christ and Krishna—and all of them pointed to the same path—renunciation. At once Ramdas made up his mind to give up for the sake of Ram, all that he till then hugged to his bosom as his own, and leave the *samsaric*[3] world. During this period, he was very simple in his dress, which consisted of a piece of cloth covering the upper part of the body and another wound round the lower part. Next day, he got two clothes of this kind dyed in *gerrua* or red ochre, and the same night wrote two letters—one to his wife, whom Ram had made him look upon for some time past as his sister[4]—and another to a kind friend whom Ram had brought in touch with Ramdas for his deliverance from debts. The resolution was made. At five o'clock in the morning he bade farewell to a world for which he had lost all attraction and in which he could find nothing to call his own. The body, the mind, the soul—all were laid at the feet of Ram—that Eternal Being, full of love and full of mercy.

---

[1] *sloka*: verse
[2] *avatar*: divine incarnation
[3] *samsaric*: pertaining to the illusory nature of conditioned life
[4] This letter is in the Appendix

3.

Adoption of Sannyas[1]

THE MORNING TRAIN carried Ramdas away from Mangalore and dropped him in the evening at Erode—a railway junction. He had taken with him a sum of Rupees 25 and a few books including the Gita and the New Testament. At Erode he found himself strangely helpless without any plans or thought for the future. He did not know where he was being led by Ram. He wandered about for some time and when darkness fell, he approached a small, low hut on the roadside and, finding at its entrance a middle-aged mother[2], requested her to give him some food. The kind mother at once welcomed him into her hut and served him with some rice and curds. The mother was very kind. With great difficulty could she be induced to accept some money for the food supplied by her.

On leaving the hut, he proceeded to the railway station. He laid himself down on a corner in the station and took rest for some time. He did not know what to do or where to go. At midnight, a bell rang to announce the arrival of a train. He got up and found near him a Tamilian who inquired of him regarding his movements. Ramdas was unable to say anything in reply. Ram alone could determine his future. Here this friend promised Ramdas to take him with him as far as Trichinopoly, for which place he was bound. Money was given him for the purchase of a ticket for Ramdas, and both boarded the train.

---
[1] *sannyas*: religious renunciation, monkhood
[2] In India saints and seekers commonly regard all women as mothers

It was evening when the train reached Trichinopoly station. Alighting from the train, he proceeded to the city. All the time, all the way from Mangalore, the divine *mantram* of Sri Ram was on his lips. He could never forget it. The utterance of Ram's name alone sustained and cheered him. Taking rest for the night on the veranda of a house by the roadside, next morning he started on foot to Srirangam about seven miles from Trichy. He reached the place at about 8 o'clock.

Here Ramdas was first let into the secret of Ram's purpose in drawing him out from the sphere of his former life and surroundings—and that purpose was to take him on a pilgrimage to sacred shrines and holy rivers. At Srirangam the beautiful river Kaveri was flowing in all her purity and majesty. Going up to the river, he bathed in its clear waters. Here on the banks of the Kaveri he assumed, by Ram's command, the robe of a *sannyasin*[3]. It was a momentous step by taking which Ram gave him an entirely new birth. The white clothes previously worn by him were offered up to the Kaveri—who carried them away in her rushing waters. The *gerrua* or orange-colored clothes were put on and the following prayer went up to the feet of Almighty Ram:

O Ram! O Love Infinite—Protector of all the worlds! It is by Thy wish alone that Thy humble slave has been induced to adopt *sannyas*. In Thy name alone, O Ram, he has given up *samsara*[4], and cut asunder all bonds, all ties.

O Ram, bless Thy poor devotee with Thy grace. May Ramdas be endued with strength, courage and faith to carry out in Thy name, Ram, the following vows and bear all trials and all kinds of privations that may beset the path of a *sannyasi* in his passage through the rough and perilous life of a mendicant:

1. This life be henceforth entirely consecrated to meditation and the service of Sri Ram.

2. Strict celibacy be observed, looking upon all women as mothers.

3. The body be maintained and fed upon the food procured by *bhiksha* or on what was offered as alms.

---

[3] *sannyasin*: travelling monk
[4] *samsara*: impermanent, worldly life

4.

SRIRANGAM

THE THRILLS of a new birth, a new life, with the sweet love of Ram was felt. A peace came upon Ramdas' struggling soul. The turmoil ceased. Ram's own hands seemed to have touched the head of his slave—Ram blessed. O tears, flow on, for the mere joy of a deliverance! Sorrow, pain, anxiety and care—all vanished, never to return. All glory to Thee, Ram. The great blessing came from Ram: "I take thee under my guidance and protection—remain ever my devotee—thy name shall be Ramdas."

Yes, Ramdas, what a grand privilege it is to become the *das*[1] of Ram who is all love—kindness—all mercy—all forgiveness!

Now, he came up to a *dharmashala*[2] close to the river and found some sadhus[3] sitting on the floor of the passage leading out to the main road. They were busy performing *Ram-bhajan* to the accompaniment of cymbals and *ektar*. They were singing the glorious name of Ram. Ramdas also squatted beside the two young *sannyasis* and placed his *lota*[4]—procured at Trichy—in front of him to receive *bhiksha*[5] from the pilgrims, who passed that way after their bath. The *bhajan*[6] of the two young devotees was really very sweet. Time passed

---
[1] *das*: servant, often in the sense of servant of God
[2] *dharmashala*: way station for pilgrims
[3] *sadhu*: monk, often wandering
[4] *lota*: water container
[5] *bhiksha*: alms
[6] *bhajan*: devotional singing

most pleasantly. It was about twelve noon that the *bhajan* came to a close. Looking upon the cloth spread in front of them, the young sadhus observed only three quarter *anna*[7] pieces lying on it—all they had got for the day. With a disappointed look one of them remarked:

"Since morning we have been singing the glory of God and He has given us only this much. Hunger is pinching the stomach. How are we to procure food, O God? Is Thy *bhajan* from morning till now worth only nine *pies*[8]?"

This question was at once answered by Ramdas: "No, young brothers, no value can be set upon your *bhajan*. God is always kind and loving. He never forsakes those who depend upon Him. Ram has sent through His humble slave money for your food today."

So saying, he dropped into the hands of the sadhus one rupee out of the amount he was then carrying with him. The poor sadhus simply stared at him in amazement. Their eyes were filled with tears. They exclaimed:

"O God, Thy ways are wonderful—pardon, pardon Thy unworthy slaves, we doubted Thee and Thy love. In future, grant that we may never blame Thee, but bear all sufferings patiently in Thy name."

The sadhus then left the place. Looking into his own *lota* Ramdas discovered in it two *pies*. His heart leaped with joy at the sight of these tiny coins—the first proceeds of his *bhiksha*! Buying two small plantains with the coins he ate them with all pleasure. At this time in the same line in which he was sitting there was another sadhu on the right—whilst the young sadhus aforementioned were on his left. Now, this sadhu coming forward enquired as to where Ramdas was proceeding. He could not, of course, find a reply to this question. Ram alone could do so. Receiving no reply, the sadhu proposed to take Ramdas with him to Rameshwaram whither he was going.

---

[7] *anna*: 1/16th of a rupee
[8] *pies*: 1/64th of a rupee (rhymes with nice)

O Ram, Thy kindness is indeed very great. To guide Thy helpless slave Thou hast sent to him this sadhu—why? He can be taken to be none other than Ram Himself.

From time to time Ramdas met sadhus—who not only led him on the pilgrimage but also took every care of him. All these sadhus, shall, by Ram's will, go by one name, "sadhu-Ram[9]."

---

[9] *sadhu–Ram*: literally God in the form of sadhu

5.

Rameshwaram

The guide was at once accepted. Ramdas had then with him about rupees 9, which amount he handed over to the sadhu-Ram and felt much relieved by doing so. To carry money is to carry anxiety with you; for it draws your attention to it now and again. On making over the money, he suggested to the sadhu-Ram to get the rupees changed into one *anna* coins and have them all distributed to the poor who were begging at the doors of temples, and this desire he carried out. Now, Ramdas threw himself more completely than ever on the support of Ram with only two clothes and a few books—all his possessions in the world. He started with the sadhu-Ram whom Ram had sent as a guide. He led him to the railway station and both got into a train running to Rameshwaram. No ticket—Ram was ticket and all in all.

Whilst in the train, Ramdas continued his meditation of Ram. The train travelled on until it reached a station about six miles from Rameshwaram. Here a ticket inspector came into the compartment in which Ramdas and his kind guide were seated. After checking the tickets of other passengers, he approached the sadhus and cried, "Tickets—Tickets."

"No tickets, brother, we are sadhus," was the reply.

"Without tickets you cannot travel any farther. You have to get down here," said the Inspector.

At once getting up, Ramdas told the sadhu-Ram that it was Ram's wish that they should alight at that place. Walking out of the station they came to the high road. Here the Saduram grumbled over the action of the Inspector. To this Ramdas said:

"Brother, we cannot travel all along to Rameshwaram by train. Pilgrimages should be made on foot. But somehow Ram was kind enough to take us on the train so far. We have only to walk a distance of six miles in order to reach Rameshwaram. It is the will of Ram that this distance should be covered on foot. Be cheerful, brother."

They started to walk. When they travelled about two miles Ram brought them in touch with a barber. Till then, since he started from Mangalore, Ramdas had not had a shave. So, here, he first got his beard, mustache and head all shaved after the manner of *sannyasis*. As they were nearing Rameshwaram, they came to a tank[1] by the roadside named Lakshman Kund. After bathing in this tank they passed by a number of small tanks, bearing different names.

At last Ram directed their steps to the famous temple of Rameshwaram. The temple is a gigantic structure. One actually loses oneself in the bewildering passages, corridors and aisles that lead to the place of worship. When the sadhus approached the Holy of Holies they found the door open—the worship of Rameshwar was going on in all its ceremonial eclat. O Ram! All glory to Thee! The occasion and the place sent thrills of joy into Ramdas' soul. Here Ramdas came in touch with some *mahatmas*[2] who had come there on pilgrimage, of whom one, Swami Govindanand, was very kind to him. The Swami said that he belonged to the *Mutt*[3] of Sri Siddharudha Swami of Hubli and offered an invitation to Ramdas to attend the *Shivaratri* festival in the Hubli Mutt, which was then shortly to take place.

---

[1] *tank*: pond, often artificially constructed
[2] *mahatma*: literally "great soul"
[3] *mutt*: monastery or religious center

6.

MADURA[1]

RAMDAS REMAINED in Rameshwaram for two days. The sadhu-Ram then proposing a move led him to the railway station. Catching a train proceeding further south, they reached a place called Dhanushkodi. On alighting here, the sadhu-Ram—the guide so kindly provided by Ram—walked in the direction of the sea with Ramdas at his heels. Ramdas who was always busy with the meditation of Ram was feeling as though he was moving about in a dream—Ram, his sole Quest, sole Thought, sole Aim. It was about two mile's walk to the spot on the seashore where legend declares Sri Ramachandra built the celebrated *sethu* or bridge during His excursion to Lanka. Half way on the sands it began to drizzle. The season was cold, clothing was scanty, but Ram's kindness and grace were very great. Going down to the extreme south of this projecting piece of sandy land, both bathed in the sea.

Next, the sadhu-Ram and Ramdas went to a small temple close by where they had the *darshan*[2] of two sadhus permanently residing there. A brisk walk back to Dhanushkodi brought them to a *dharmashala* where the sadhu-Ram provided Ramdas and himself with some food. Ramdas was at this time only on a fruit diet or food without salt and chilies.

After a day's stay here they started by train for Madura and reached the place in due time. The temple of Madura was

---
[1] Now called Madurai
[2] *darshan*: blessing of being in presence of holy person, place or object

visited. The temple of Meenakshi is a beautiful pile wherein the sculptor has exhibited all his skill. The life-size symmetrical images cut in stone seem to be stepping out of the broad pillars that support the upper structure of the temple. The shrine is massive in build and can stand the wear and tear of ages. The sight of it is, in brief, a most imposing one.

Here Ramdas met again Swami Govindananda who was so kind to him at Rameshwaram. He with two other saints found Ramdas sitting on one side of the entrance to the temple. The tired sadhu-Ram—Ramdas' guide—was sleeping and Ramdas was squatting at his feet. In sleep the sadhu-Ram's legs happened to touch Ramdas' body. Swami Govindananda remonstrated at this and was about to shake up the sadhu-Ram when Ramdas addressed the Swami:

"Maharaj—please don't disturb the sadhu. He is sound asleep."

"Behold!" cried the Swami, "He is kicking at you. I cannot bear the sight. I consider it as nothing short of sacrilege."

"Swamiji, it is all right," replied Ramdas. "His feet are holy. He is Ramdas' *Guru*[3]. He is Ram—so no harm anyway."

The Swami said that he could not quite understand Ramdas, whom he held in high reverence.

Next day, the sadhu-Ram proposed a move from the place. Before doing so he told Ramdas that his duty, in so far as guiding him to Rameshwaram was concerned, was over and that he should be permitted to part from him in order to proceed to his *Gurustan*[4] at Rajamannargudi. All along, the sadhu-Ram had been very kind to him and had looked after him very tenderly at all stages of the journey, taking every care of him. At a certain railway junction, he left Ramdas. However, before doing so, he assured Ramdas that the train was carrying him to Chidambaram, a noted shrine.

---

[3] *guru*: spiritual preceptor
[4] *gurustan*: abode of his guru

7.

Chidambaram

AT NOON, THE TRAIN steamed into Chidambaram station. Ramdas stepped out on the platform. He was now without a guide. Ram had made him a child, without plans, without any thought of the next moment, but with his mind ever fixed in the one thought of Ram, Ram. He found some pilgrims proceeding towards the city and followed them. At midday he reached the precincts of the temple of Chidambaram. He went up straight to the entrance of the temple, but could not gain admission as none was allowed to get in without a payment of *annas* 4—the entrance fee. He was without a single *pie* which, however, he did not at all regret. He wandered for a time amidst the ruins surrounding the temple and, after bathing in one of the many tanks, seated himself on a long stone in the sun, in a secluded portion of the ruins. It was now about 1 o'clock. Ramdas, who was all the while absorbed in the *Ram Japa*[1], opened his small bundle of books and, taking out the *Bhagavad Gita*, commenced reading it. He had not perused half a dozen verses when he found a stout Tamilian coming towards him and taking a seat beside him.

"Maharaj," he inquired, "may I know if you have taken any food for the day?"

"No," replied Ramdas, "but Ram provides. No fear so far, no thought of it, you remind me, friend."

---
[1] *Ram Japa*: repeating the Name of God

"Can you tell me what kind of food you take?" next asked the friend.

"Plantains, if you please," Ramdas rejoined.

At once the friend got up and disappeared, and in a short time returned with a dozen plantains, and laying them in front of Ramdas, pressed him to eat. O Ram, Thy ways are wonderful! The repast over, the Tamilian, who was sent by Ram Himself to look after the wants of his humble devotee, next asked Ramdas to follow him. At the entrance of the temple he paid *annas* 8, the entrance fee for both, and took him inside the temple. After the *darshan* of the idols, he showed him the whole interior of the temple. One rarity here is, the roof of the central building of the temple is covered with sheets of gold. The guide furnished by Ram was very kind to him. There was that night, *puja*[2] in the temple in a grand style, and also a procession attended by thousands. When all this was over, it was past midnight; the Tamilian friend secured for Ramdas a place for spending the night. Here he made Ramdas understand that he was only a pilgrim come there to attend that night's *puja* and procession from a neighboring town, and that he intended to return by the early morning train, and that he was much blessed by Ramdas' society for ever so short a time. Ramdas' heart was too full for words. Ram's kindness was indescribable.

Next morning, along with other pilgrims, Ramdas came to the railway station. But where to go and by what train, he was entirely in the dark. His imaginative faculty for making plans and seeking information was totally absent. Without a guide he was feeling helpless. He depended for all things on Ram whom he was remembering every moment of his existence. On reaching the station he found a train standing, but did not know whence it had come and whither it was proceeding. He straightaway went up to the gate and was entering the platform when the ticket clerk barred his passage

---

[2]*puja*: worship

telling him that he should not enter without a ticket. It was all Ram's will. Ram did not want that he should travel by this train. Probably it might be running towards a direction where Ramdas would come across no places of pilgrimage. Ram knew best.

8.

JOURNEY TO TIRUPAPULIYUR

A LITTLE DISTANCE from the station, under a tree, were piled up some stones. Ramdas, going up to the place, sat down on them and continued his meditation of Ram. It was past midday when another train arrived. Ramdas leaving the place, got upon the platform, nobody obstructing him at the gate this time, because this train was the right one for him to travel in. Here he came in touch with a sadhu who immediately took him up. Ram gave him another guide. Both entered the carriage. The new sadhu–Ram was very solicitous. He asked him as to where he intended going. Ramdas was perplexed at this question. The simple truth was, he did not know. He replied:

"Ram knows, and since you are sent by Ram to guide him, you ought to know where he should go next."

The sadhu–Ram then said: "Well, I am taking you to Tirupapuliyur and thence to Tiruvannamalai."

"As you please," replied Ramdas. "You are Ram. Ramdas follows wherever you take him."

Now the train was running. On the front seat facing Ramdas were seated two young Hindus—English educated. Both of them stared for some time at the strange, careless and quaint *sannyasi*, that is Ramdas in front of them. Then one of them remarked to the other in English (they thought that the *sannyasi* before them was ignorant of the English language):

"Mark closely the sadhu facing us. He belongs, take my word, to a class of *sannyasis* who are perfect humbugs. The fellow has adopted this mode of life simply as a means of eking out his livelihood. This man is a veritable imposter and a hoax."

This observation was highly approved of by the other party who held a similar opinion of poor Ramdas. They spoke something more which he could not clearly catch owing to the rolling sound of the running train. O Ram, how kind of Thee to put Ramdas in a situation in which he is made to hear himself spoken of in this manner! Instead of feeling annoyed, he sent up a prayer to Ram to bless the young men for their frankness. Further, Ramdas could not resist the expression of his gratitude to these friends, and thus addressed them with hands folded in salute:

"O kind friends! It gives Ramdas great pleasure to confess that he is in full agreement with the view you have expressed about him. It is perfectly true that he is a fraud. He has simply put on the robes of a *sannyasi* in order to find a living thereby. But one thing more you discover in him and that is, he is mad of Ram and every moment he cries out to Him to make him pure and only live for Ram's sake. Besides, it is his humble presumption that Ram is taking him on this pilgrimage to purify him."

This speech surprised both the friends, not so much on account of its import as the knowledge it brought them that the vagrant *sannyasi* could understand English and therefore had grasped the purport of their remarks, which were never intended to be known to him. A sudden change came over them and both fell at his feet and sought his pardon for their "thoughtless remarks" as they termed them. Thereafter, they became very solicitous and kind. They inquired if he required anything to eat. This was a reminder to him that he had not tasted anything the whole of that day, a circumstance which he had entirely forgotten. He then told the two friends that he was mainly living upon fruits, and would gladly accept any alms from them. After some consultation with the sadhu–Ram—the guide, they handed over to him some money for the purchase of fruits for Ramdas. Ram's ways are indeed inscrutable—He is all love and all kindness!

9.

Pondicherry and Tiruvannamalai

IN DUE COURSE, Tirupapuliyur was reached and Ramdas was taken by the sadhu-Ram to the house of an old relation of his, where, on the veranda, the night was spent. Next morning, the sadhu-Ram advised him to go for alms to a few houses pointed out by him.

"Look here, Maharaj," said the kind-hearted sadhu-Ram, "money is wanted for your plantains and milk. Ordinary food can be easily procured, but, for your food, money is needed." He conducted Ramdas to a street, both sides of which were studded with houses owned by *vakils*[1].

"Go from house to house, they might give you something. I shall wait for you at the other corner," suggested the sadhu-Ram.

Ramdas, who was always at the bidding of his guide, did as directed. Begging at the door of about half a dozen houses, he got a handful of copper and other coins which were all handed over to the sadhu-Ram who on counting found them to be about 10 *annas*.

"Your Ram is really kind," remarked the sadhu-Ram, smiling. "This sum will do for two days."

In the course of the day, there was a talk about Pondicherry, which, Ramdas came to know, lay only at a distance of about twenty miles from Tirupapuliyur. A desire sprang up in

---
[1] *vakil*: lawyer

his mind to visit the place for the *darshan* of Sri Aurobindo—the great Bengali saint. The wish was expressed to the sadhu–Ram and he agreed to it at once. The following morning early before sunrise, both started, of course on foot, and went towards Pondicherry. At about 2 p.m. the outskirts of the city of Pondicherry were reached. The peculiarity here was that the entrance to the city was lined on both sides, a few yards from each other, by toddy shops[2]! On entering the city, inquiries were made for the home or *ashram*[3] in which saint Sri Aurobindo lived. After knocking about for some time, the gate of a palatial building was pointed at by a friend, wherein, the sadhus were told, the saint was residing. Entering, Ramdas inquired of two young Bengalis, whom he met in one of the rooms at the entrance of the building, if saint Sri Aurobindo could be seen then. To this one of them replied:

"Sir, sorry, since Sri Aurobindo is in retirement, he will not give audience to anybody for a year to come."

Ramdas then begged the favor of a mere sight of the great man which would satisfy him. Even this favor could not be granted. It was all Ram's wish. So he came out and explained the circumstances to the sadhu–Ram who was waiting outside. While this was going on, a policeman was observed to be approaching the spot where the sadhus were standing. Coming up to them, the ubiquitous policeman said:

"Friends, you are wanted at the police station. You have to follow me."

At this, the sadhu–Ram was immensely frightened and pulling Ramdas aside, whispered to him that most probably the policeman was taking them to be flogged. Ramdas suggested that they might accompany the policeman and leave the future in the hands of Ram. About half a mile's walk and the police station was reached, and the sadhus found themselves standing in front of a tall man of middle age with fierce looks and a well-curved and twisted mustache. He spoke something

---
[2] *toddy*: country palm liquor
[3] *ashram*: monastery or religious center, often started by a saint

sternly, which could not be grasped, for he must have done so in French. A reply in English was given by Ramdas and the man, who seemed to be a Police Inspector, simply stared in return to indicate that he did not understand what was spoken. Then, a talk in Tamil ensued between him and the sadhu–Ram. The import of what the Police Inspector said was that only two hours were allowed for the sadhus to clear out of the city. At this, the sadhu–Ram remonstrated that after a walk of 20 miles at a stretch, the tired pilgrims required some rest and they preferred to remain in the city for the night and leave the place next morning. This reply not only did not satisfy the Inspector but also appeared to have offended him a bit. For now he talked fast, his eyes glistening and his hands twisting his mustache furiously.

The allowance of two hours was reduced to one hour, and, if they did not obey the orders promptly, he warned that they would be made to pay for it. This time the words he spoke were freely spiced here and there with some finely selected epithets of abuse. The sadhu–Ram at once pressed Ramdas to move away swiftly from that place for very life. He was, poor man, both frightened and annoyed at the sharp words of the Inspector. A few yards off the station and the sadhu–Ram commenced to pour quite a shower of abuse on the Inspector. No amount of persuasion on the part of Ramdas for peace would stop the brisk play of his tongue. He was assured it was all Ram's wish and so there was no reason to grumble. Still, he continued to give vent to choice epithets of abuse. He seemed to be quite a master in that line. For about a mile the sadhu–Ram's wrath did not cool down. Gradually, he became silent, maybe, due to exhaustion of his stock of vocabulary or on account of an empty stomach, or it might have been all a trick of Ram to test Ramdas if he would join him in the game set on foot by Him! Ram alone knows and He alone can judge.

Retracing about four miles from the city of Pondicherry, the sadhu–Ram selected the veranda of a shop which was shut, for taking rest for the night. Early the following morning they started on their return journey to Tirupapuliyur, which place they reached at 2 o'clock in the afternoon. Here it should be stated that the sadhu-Ram was looking after him so tenderly that he was a veritable foster mother to him. Again, it was all Ram's work, whose ways are at once loving and mysterious. Next day, the train carried both the sadhus to Tiruvannamalai. Here the sadhu-Ram conducted him to the house of a goldsmith with whom he was acquainted. The goldsmith was a pious man. He pressed both the sadhus to remain in his house as guests. For some days, Ramdas occupied a closed veranda in this friend's house for his meditation and rest. In the mornings and evenings he, along with the sadhu-Ram, would go to the huge temple of Mahadev[4].

One day, the kind sadhu-Ram took him for the *darshan* of a famous saint of the place, named Sri Ramana Maharshi. His *ashram* was at the foot of the Tiruvannamalai mountains. It was a thatched shed. Both the visitors entered the *ashram*, and meeting the saint, fell prostrate at his holy feet. It was really a blessed place where that great man lived. He was young but there was on his face a calmness, and in his large eyes a passionless look of tenderness, which cast a spell of peace and joy on all those who came to him. Ramdas was informed that the saint knew English. So he addressed him thus:

"Maharaj, here stands before thee a humble slave. Have pity on him. His only prayer to thee is to give him thy blessing."

The Maharshi, turning his beautiful eyes towards Ramdas, and looking intently for a few minutes into his eyes as though he was pouring into Ramdas his blessing through those orbs, shook his head to say that he had blessed. A thrill of inexpressible joy coursed through the frame of Ramdas, his whole body quivering like a leaf in the breeze. O Ram, what a love is Thine! Bidding farewell to the *mahatma* the sadhu-Ram and he returned to the goldsmith's residence.

---

[4] *Mahadev*: Lord Shiva

10.

IN THE CAVE

NOW, AT THE PROMPTING of Ram, Ramdas desiring to remain in solitude for some time, placed the matter before the sadhu-Ram. The sadhu-Ram was ever ready to fulfil his wishes. Losing no time, he took Ramdas up the mountain behind the great temple. Climbing high up, he showed him many caves. Of these, one small cave was selected for Ramdas which he occupied the next day. In this cave he lived for nearly a month in deep meditation of Ram. This was the first time he was taken by Ram into solitude for His *bhajan*. Now, he felt most blissful sensations since he could here hold undisturbed communion with Ram. He was actually rolling in a sea of indescribable happiness. To fix the mind on that fountain of bliss—Ram— means to experience pure joy!

Once, during the day, when he was lost in the madness of Ram's meditation, he came out of the cave and found a man standing a little away from the mouth of the cave. Unconsciously, he ran up to him and locked him up in a fast embrace. This action on the part of Ramdas thoroughly frightened the friend who thought that it was a mad man who was behaving in this manner and so was afraid of harm from him. It was true, he was mad—yes, he was mad of Ram, but it was a harmless madness which fact the visitor realized later. The irresistible attraction felt by him towards this friend was due to the perception of Ram in him. "O Ram, Thou art come, Thou art come!" With this thought Ramdas had run up to him. At times he would feel driven to clasp in his arms the very trees and plants growing in the vicinity of the cave. Ram was attracting him from all directions. Oh, the mad and loving attraction of Ram! O Ram, Thou art Love, Light and Bliss. Thus passed his days in that cave.

For food, he would come down in the morning and, going into the city, beg from door to door and receive from the kind mothers of the place handfuls of rice in his small *lota*. When the *lota* was a little over half-full, he would return to the cave. Collecting some dry twigs, he would light a fire over which he would boil the rice in the same *lota*. Water was at hand. A small stream of pure, crystal water was flowing down the hill just in front of the cave, and in this stream it was also most refreshing to take the daily bath. This boiled rice was taken to appease hunger, without salt or anything else, and only once a day. To share with him in this simple fare, a number of squirrels would visit the cave. Fearlessly, at times, they would eat from his hands. Their fellowship was also a source of great joy to Ramdas. Everyday he would wander over the hills amidst the shrubs, trees and rocks—a careless, thoughtless child of Ram! It was altogether a simple and happy life that he led in that mountain retreat. The kind-hearted sadhu-Ram would meet him everyday, either up the hill or in the city, when he came down for *bhiksha*. A day came when he received Ram's command to leave the place—whereto, Ram alone knew.

11.

TIRUPATI

ONE EARLY MORNING at about 4 a.m., descending from the mountain, Ramdas walked straight to the railway station, and finding a train waiting, got on to the platform without being obstructed, and entered a compartment. A few minutes later the train moved. Where was the train taking him? It was none of his concern to try to know this. Ram never errs and a complete trust in Him means full security and the best guidance. The train ran up to the Katpadi junction. Here, Ram brought him in touch with a sadhu–Ram to guide him. He promised to take him to Tirupati, in which direction the train was running. O Ram, Thy plans are, indeed, always mysteriously worked out. The new sadhu–Ram and he travelled together, and in due course both alighted at the Tirupati station. After refreshing themselves with some food prepared by the kind-hearted sadhu–Ram, they directed their steps towards the Tirupati hill. Both commenced ascending the stone steps of the hill. It was climbing "higher still and higher up the mount of glory!" About 700 steps were covered and the sadhus reached the top of the hill at about eight in the evening. Then, they had to walk about three miles over almost level ground. It was a moonlit night but the cold up there was intense, while, at the same time, Ram's grace was correspondingly very great.

A little before midnight the temple of Balaji[1] was reached.

---
[1] *Balaji*: a form of Vishnu

At the entrance to the temple was a fire, around which a number of people were sitting. The shivering sadhus hastened to the spot, pressed themselves in among these friends and warmed their hands and feet. Ram was indeed kind! A short time later, the door-keeper of the temple commanded all at the fire to leave the place and get out since it was time to close the main door of the temple. So, all had to give up the fireside most reluctantly. The sadhu-Ram requested the watchman to permit himself and Ramdas to spend the night inside the temple, which request was not granted. It was all Ram's will. To come out of the temple meant complete exposure to the strong and extremely cold breeze blowing over the hills. It was dark now and they had to search out a place to rest for the night. There were some massive buildings—*dharmashalas*, all open. However, the sadhus scrambled into one of these and settled themselves down. The sadhu-Ram began to grumble at the cold, and said:

"Swami, it is impossible to think of sleep for the night. The cold will not allow us a wink of sleep."

"So much the better," replied Ramdas. "All the time can then be devoted to *Ram-bhajan*—the *bhajan* of that All-powerful and All-loving Being."

"That is all right for you," remarked the sadhu-Ram, "but I should suggest a move from this place as soon as the day breaks. One more night in this plight shall certainly stiffen us into sheer logs of wood."

Receiving no reply from Ramdas who was then engaged in the meditation of Ram, the sadhu-Ram laid himself down, and twisted himself into the shape of the figure 8, at the same time covering his body with a thin cotton cloth, the only spare cloth he had. This cloth was too small to fully cover him in spite of his assuming a position in which his bent knees were drawn up to touch his very nose.

"Sleep is quite out of the question," again said the sadhu-Ram.

Poor friend, Ram was sorely testing him, all for his good

Poor friend, Ram was sorely testing him, all for his good and good alone. The night passed. Early morning, when the day was breaking, the shivering sadhu proposed a climb down the hill. But Ramdas suggested that they might go farther on about three miles and visit the waterfall called "Papanasini." The general belief is that the person who takes a bath in this waterfall will be washed of all his or her sins—hence the name. The sadhu–Ram agreeing, both proceeded to this spot and bathed in the waters falling down a rock with great force. Since it was broad daylight now, the top of the hill in all directions was seen clearly. The beautiful landscapes and valleys that met the eyes were simply entrancing. Bath over, the sadhu–Ram hastened down the hill, followed by Ramdas, and before evening they reached the city below. The same evening, both boarded a train running northwards.

12.

GOD IS EVERYWHERE

THEY TRAVELLED to Kalahasti. After a day's stay here, they left for Jagannath Puri. It was noon; the sadhu-Ram and Ramdas were in the train. A ticket inspector, a Christian, dressed in European fashion, stepped into the carriage at a small station, and coming up to the sadhus asked for tickets.

"Sadhus carry no tickets, brother, for they neither possess nor care to possess any money," said Ramdas in English.

The ticket inspector replied: "You can speak English. Educated as you are, you cannot travel without a ticket. I have to ask you both to get down."

The sadhu-Ram and he accordingly got down at the bidding of the inspector. "It is all Ram's will," assured Ramdas to his guide.

They were now on the platform and there was still some time for the train to start. The ticket inspector, meanwhile, felt an inclination to hold conversation with Ramdas who, with the sadhu-Ram, was waiting for the train to depart.

"Well," broke in the inspector looking at Ramdas, "may I know with what purpose you are travelling in this manner?"

"In quest of God," was his simple reply.

"They say God is everywhere," persisted the inspector. "Then, where is the fun of your knocking about in search of Him, while He is at the very place from which you started on this quest, as you say?"

"Right, brother," replied Ramdas. "God is everywhere but he wants to have this fact actually proved by going to all places and realizing His presence everywhere."

"Well then," continued the inspector, "if you are discovering God wherever you go, you must be seeing Him here, on this spot, where you stand."

"Certainly, brother," rejoined Ramdas. "He is here at the very place where we stand."

"Can you tell me where he is?" asked the inspector.

"Behold, He is here, standing in front of me!" exclaimed Ramdas enthusiastically.

"Where, where?" cried the inspector impatiently.

"Here, here!" pointed Ramdas smiling, and patted on the broad chest of the inspector himself. "In the tall figure standing in front, that is, in yourself, Ramdas clearly sees God who is everywhere."

For a time, the inspector looked confused. Then he broke into a hearty fit of laughter. Opening the door of the compartment from which he had asked the sadhus to get down, he requested them to get in again, and they did so, followed by him. He sat in the train with the sadhus for some time.

"I cannot disturb you, friends, I wish you all success in your quest of God." With these words he left the carriage and the train rolled onwards. O Ram, Thy name be glorified!

13.

A Kind Policeman

AT NOON, NEXT DAY, Ram, who is the loving Parent of all, seeing that the sadhus were going without food, induced a ticket clerk to ask them to alight at a station between Bezwada and Jagannath Puri. Ramdas does not remember the name of the station. Coming out of the station, they proceeded towards the city and procuring some food, refreshed themselves and, returning in the evening to the same station, spent the night there. Next day, they had to catch the train at the same hour at which they were made to alight the previous day. Well, there was some difficulty to encounter—all, of course, apparent, for Ram's ways are always mysterious. It was agreed to by both the ticket clerk and the stationmaster not to permit these sadhus to board the train. So, on the arrival of the train, when the sadhus were entering the carriage, both these officers, of course, in strict discharge of their duties, prevented them from doing so, in spite of the entreaties of the sadhu-Ram. The passengers on the platform had all occupied the carriages. The two sadhus and the railway officers were alone on the platform. The clerk and the stationmaster were keenly watching the sadhus lest they should slip into the train. O Ram, how wonderful Thou art! There was still some time for the train to start. Now a railway policeman coming up to the sadhus, asked them to get into a carriage. But the sadhu-Ram told him that the ticket clerk would not allow them to go. The policeman then, going to the place where the clerk and the stationmaster were standing, placed the case of the sadhus before them, saying:

"You see, these *sannyasis* deserve to be allowed to get into the train. As regards tickets, they cannot be expected to carry money since money is not their quest, as in the case of worldly people."

These words did not convince the railway officers. They replied, rightly of course:

"It is against rules to permit anybody to travel in the train without a ticket. So, it is useless on your part to plead for them. Moreover, you forget the fact that your suggestion is against the very spirit of your duty as a policeman in the service of the railway company."

This reply annoyed the policeman considerably. He felt strongly that these sadhus must, somehow, be allowed to travel by the train.

It was now nearly time for the train to start. The kind policeman was very uneasy. His eyes flared up and there was a glint of a desperate look in them. He swiftly moved towards the train and opening the door of the carriage, beckoned the sadhus to enter, which they did, as told. It was all the work of a moment. But this was observed by the ticket clerk from a distance, and he ran up to the place at once.

"On what authority did you permit the sadhus to enter the train?" questioned the clerk in an angry tone.

The policeman, who was tall and stalwart, placed himself in front of the closed door of the carriage, his back leaning against it.

"Look here, brother," he replied in a cool but firm voice, "in a matter of this kind, there is no higher authority than the dictates of one's own conscience, which are rightly considered as the promptings of God Himself."

"This action of yours shall be reported to the higher authorities and you will answer for it!" warned the ticket clerk.

"Certainly friend," replied the policeman" As a result of your report, even if I be dismissed from the service, I am fully prepared to face all consequences. But neither you nor anybody on earth shall prevent the sadhus from travelling by this train."

The clerk was sorely perplexed at the attitude of the policeman, and was looking for the stationmaster, who was then busy giving the signal for the departure of the train, since the time was up. The whistle went and the train rolled on. The clerk was simply staring at the carriage occupied by the sadhus, quite helpless. O Ram! What can poor Ramdas, Thy slave, understand by this incident? Why, when Thy omnipotent hands are at work, nothing can stop or obstruct Thee. O kind and loving Protector of the universe! Thy one touch can change in a moment the entire face of the universe! The very policeman, who is stationed on the railway platform to prevent passengers from breaking the rules of the company, deliberately breaks all such rules himself and seats two sadhus in the train, knowing full well that they held no tickets, and this too in face of bitter opposition and at the risk of losing his job! O Ram, it is now beyond any doubt that Thou art seated in the hearts of all, inducing the whole universe to act and move in strict accordance with Thy sovereign will. Ram! Thou art indeed the true lover of Thy devotees. Thy slave cannot find words to express Thy greatness and Thy love! O tears, flow on! And this is the only way Ramdas can express his feelings.

14.

JAGANNATH PURI

THE TRAIN RODE ON. Jagannath Puri was reached in the evening. The night was spent on the veranda of a *dharmashala*. The cold here was also very great. Next morning, both went up to a large tank outside the city, and finishing bath and ablutions directed their steps to the famous temple of Jagannath, the beautiful white dome of which was visible high up in the sky from any place in that pious city. Now the sadhu–Ram and Ramdas found themselves at the great door of the temple. But how to gain entrance? The doorway was completely blocked up by the rushing crowd of pilgrims. There was a good deal of elbowing, pushing and kicking in the thick and struggling mass of humanity. Looking on this state of things, Ramdas, with hands joined in salutation, spoke thus:

O Ram! How can Thy poor slave gain access in this rush of men and obtain Thy *darshan*? There appears to be no chance for him—a weak and helpless *fakir*[1].

Scarcely were these words uttered, when from the crowd at the entrance, out came a tall *Brahmin*[2] and approaching him, took him by the hand, led him to the door, and using all his strength he pressed himself through the thick crowd, and making a passage, conducted the bewildered Ramdas along with him. It all appeared like a dream! Ramdas had now become unconscious of his body and plunged into communion

---
[1] *fakir*: ascetic or mendicant, often Muslim
[2] *Brahmin*: highest caste, traditionally priests

with the Almighty Ram. In about five minutes, he was standing before the big idol of Jagannath[3]. The *Brahmin* still holding him by the hand, Ramdas laid his head at the feet of this idol.

This over, the *Brahmin* took him for a round of the temple. O Ram! What words can convey Thy kindness to Thy slave! All glory to Thee! All along, while going round, he was immersed in a strange ecstasy, tears flowing down profusely from his eyes. What joy indescribable! Oh! One moment of that existence outweighs all the pleasures of the world. A few minutes later, he and the *Brahmin* guide were out again at the very place wherefrom he had been fetched. Here procuring some *prasad*[4], i.e., boiled rice, the *Brahmin* put it into the mouth of Ramdas.

"Now my work is over," said he and was going inside the temple leaving him; but before he did so, Ramdas was somehow impelled to put to him a question:

"Brother, how was it you were so kind to a wandering sadhu whom you took into the temple for *darshan*?"

"Jagannath alone can answer your question," replied the *Brahmin*. "No sooner did I see you, than a strange and sudden desire seized me to take you in and get you the *darshan* of Jagannath. Why I did all this I cannot explain—it was all the work of God." Certainly Ram's work!

---

[3] *Jagannath*: form of Krishna
[4] *prasad*: food offered to God or a saint before being eaten

15.

CHRIST, A MESSENGER OF GOD

THE SAME EVENING, the sadhu–Ram led the way to the railway station where they boarded a train. The train travelled onward north, carrying the two sadhus until it reached the station this side of the great Howrah Station. It is the rule of the railway company at this station to collect tickets from all passengers. Accordingly, an Anglo–Indian friend, a ticket collector, entered the carriage and demanded of the sadhus their tickets. The sadhus had, of course, to confess that they possessed no tickets. At this the strict ticket collector asked the sadhus to alight since he said it was against rules to travel by train without tickets. This order was promptly obeyed by both the sadhus. It was all Ram's wish. The time was about 8 o'clock in the night, and the station was a small one. They were made to stand near the gate until the train departed, when the attention of the Anglo–Indian friend was drawn to the sadhus again. Coming to them, he ordered them to sit down. At once the sadhus sat down.

"No, not there," said the friend and pointed his finger a few yards to his left. The sadhus instantly got up and going to the place indicated, sat there.

"Not there, not there," cried again the Christian friend, who seemed to possess a sense of humor. "This side," and pointing to his right, said, "get up, quick, and sit here."

The sadhus did as they were bid and occupied the new place pointed out to them. Again, for the third time, a command came from the friend for a move to another place, which was also immediately obeyed. Both the sadhus were moving about in perfect agreement. When they sat down at the last mentioned place indicated by the Anglo–Indian friend, the sadhu–Ram grumbling remarked to Ramdas:

"Swami, this is a strange man dealing with us. His only intention seems to be to tease us."

"No, brother, you mistake the kindness of this friend," replied Ramdas. "We had been so long sitting in the train and as a result, our legs had become benumbed. To remove the stiffness and to induce brisker circulation of blood, the kind friend makes us walk this side and that, and asks us to sit and stand. It is all for good. Ram be praised for His goodness and love."

This reply did not seem to satisfy the sadhu–Ram who said: "Your philosophy is very hard for a poor sadhu like myself to properly understand."

During this conversation the Christian friend had disappeared. Now he returned with a bull's eye lantern and holding it straight towards the sadhus made the light fall first on the faces of the sadhus, one after the other, and then, all over them and around them. By the help of the light, he made the discovery of the bag and brass pot of the sadhu–Ram and a small bundle of books and a tiny aluminum pot of Ramdas.

"Now I will have this." Saying thus, the friend took the brass pot of the sadhu–Ram and placed it beside him at which action the poor sadhu–Ram turned quite pale.

Next, the friend pulled his bag towards him and opening it examined its contents but finding nothing worth taking, handed it back.

"Next, what have you got?" he asked, his attention now directed towards Ramdas.

Meanwhile, Ramdas had placed his pot and the parcel of books in front of the Christian friend.

"Brother," answered Ramdas, "these two articles are yours. You are quite welcome to have them since Ramdas never owned them as his at any time; they belong to anyone who demands them."

"This small pot is not wanted," he remarked, "the brass one is more suitable. Now what is this you have in this parcel?"

On uncovering it his sight fell upon the pocket-sized New Testament on the very top of the packet. Pulling it out he looked on the title in gilt-letters—"New Testament." He questioned Ramdas:

"What have you to do with this book?"

"Everything, brother," replied Ramdas.

"Do you believe in Christ?" asked he.

"Why not? Christ is also a messenger of God—come for the salvation of mankind."

This reply at once touched the heart of the friend. Coming close to Ramdas, he said:

"Master, kindly pardon your servant who gave you a good deal of trouble without knowing you."

Saying thus, he led both inside the station and offering two chairs made them sit on them. The brass pot was, of course, returned to the sadhu-Ram which brought color and light back to his sorrowful face. O! Christ be praised. The Anglo-Indian friend became very kind and offered to get them tea, etc., all of which Ramdas declined with thanks.

"Look here, master, another train is due in about half an hour. On her arrival, I shall see that both of you are comfortably seated in it, and then you can proceed to Howrah. Again, your servant regrets very much the treatment meted out to you and sues for your pardon."

O Ram, O Christ, Thou hast a strange way of testing Thy humble slave. O Ram, Thou art a mystery, but Thou art Love—kindness itself. He who trusts Thee, O Ram, is sure of Thy entire support. This is all one can know of Thee and that is sufficient. To understand Thy ways is not only impossible but unnecessary for Thy humble devotees. To bask in the sunshine of Thy infinite love is in itself the highest happiness. The child asks for the love of the mother and gets it and is satisfied. Where is then room to ask for anything more than this?

In due time the train arrived, and the Christian friend, according to his promise, secured comfortable seats for the sadhus in a compartment. The train started and reached the Howrah Station at about 10 p.m.

16.

CALCUTTA AND DAKSHINESHWAR

BOTH THE SADHUS launched out in the darkness and coming upon the banks of the Ganges crossed the huge bridge over it. The cold was very great. Reaching the other side and turning left, they descended some steps and came to a place where a portion of a temple, close to the Ganges, is used by the *Brahmins* to attend spiritually upon the pilgrims after bath in the sacred river. Here, the sadhus found a plank on which they rested for the night. Next day, early morning, they mounted up and proceeded to Calcutta. Making enquiries about the temple of Kali[1] they were directed towards Kalighat about seven miles from the place. In due course, they reached Kalighat and went straight up to the temple and stood in front of the big image of Kali in black stone—a large red tongue lolling out of Her widened mouth.

"O Mother of the Universe," prayed Ramdas, "bless Thy weak and helpless child. May Thy humble slave look upon all womankind as mothers—representing Thy divine form." Here again Ramdas experienced a feeling of inexpressible joy and complete resignation to the divine will. Tears flowed profusely from his eyes. It was all due to the Mother's grace. The sadhus stayed in the *dharmashala* at this place for two days.

Retracing their steps back to Calcutta, the sadhus again arrived at the banks of the Ganges. As prompted by Ram,

---

[1] *Kali*: an aspect of God as Divine Mother (Primal Energy)

Ramdas then proposed to go to Dakshineshwar, and accordingly they boarded a steamboat—a kind friend having furnished them with tickets—which carried them on the breast of the Ganges, on the banks of which they alighted, a long distance away from Calcutta. This was 10 o'clock in the night. The night was dark. With some friends on the road they inquired for the way leading to Dakshineshwar, and as directed they walked on from lane to lane, and then through fields losing their way at places for want of a guide. It was all Ram's work, who was testing his devotees. However, by His grace, the sadhus reached at last the entrance to the famous temple at midnight. They found the big massive front door shut, at which they knocked. The door opened and a voice in a high key demanded:

"Who is there?"

"Two wandering sadhus come for the *darshan* of Kali," replied Ramdas.

"That is all right, you cannot come in now, you may do so tomorrow morning."

So saying the friend was about to close the door in the face of the sadhus, but both of them quietly got in, in spite of his remonstrances, and he was found later to be the night-watchman. Both the sadhus walked into the large square of the temple, fully resolved not to turn back until they obtained the *darshan* of Kali. The kind watchman, who got wild at first, softened, and told the pilgrims that they could get the *darshan* of Kali, but they must not think of staying in the temple for the night, as it was against rules to do so.

"That is Kali's affair—none of ours to think of at present," replied Ramdas.

They walked to the place whence a light was proceeding and found themselves standing in front of the image of Kali. A thrill of joy coursed through Ramdas' frame at the sight of the figure of Kali—the beau ideal of Sri Ramakrishna Paramahamsa—that well-known saint of Dakshineshwar. While they were standing with folded hands before the idol, a friend issued out of the temple and finding the sadhus, gave them some of Kali's *prasad* to eat. Ramdas then questioned if it was the wish of Mother Kali to grant them refuge for the night in the temple. The *pujari*[2]—this kind friend was such—hesitated and said:

"According to the rules of the temple no outsiders are allowed to sleep during nights inside the temple precincts. However, since it is nearly midnight now, it would be hard indeed to send you out in the darkness and cold."

O Ram! No rules, no regulations are binding upon Thy *bhaktas*[3]. To utter Thy glorious name means to be at once free from all bonds, all ties, all rules and all fetters. Then the kind *pujari* friend led the sadhus to an open *dharmashala* on the banks of the Ganges. He again provided them with some eatables and pressed them to eat. Ram's kindness knows no bounds. In the place occupied by the sadhus, sleep was out of the question. Not only was the cold very severe due to the chill breeze blowing from the river but also quite a host of mosquitos commenced attacking the sadhus in grim earnest.

"This is a terrible state of things," cried out the sadhu-Ram. "In Tirupati, there was only cold which was comparatively tolerable, but here, it is coupled with the sharp stings of mosquitoes."

"It is all right, friend," replied Ramdas. "Ram's kindness cannot be sufficiently praised. He has found a most efficient method to keep Ramdas awake to enable him to perform *Rambhajan* without sleep encroaching upon it in the least."

"Well, well," was all that the sadhu said, who was now busy driving away the winged guests by waving to and fro the piece of cloth with which he covered his body. The sadhu spent a very disturbed night, complaining, fretting and grumbling while Ramdas was struggling to bear it all by absorbing his mind in the meditation of Ram, who in a short time made him unconscious of his body, in which state he remained most of the night.

---
[2] *pujari*: temple priest
[3] *bhaktas*: devotees of God

The day was just breaking when the sadhu–Ram got up and asked Ramdas to follow him out of the place. He did not know where to go. But one thing, he wanted to be away from the place at the earliest opportunity. The sadhus had not proceeded half a furlong from the temple when they met the *pujari*, who had been so hospitable to them the previous night, coming up in front of them.

"Where are you going so early?" hailed the kindhearted friend. "You should not go away unless you take the midday meal, the *prasad* of Kali. Pray, get back to the temple."

This invitation had to be accepted, and both returned to the temple. Ram's ways are mysterious indeed!

"Wash yourselves and your clothes in the Ganges," suggested the *pujari*. "In due time, you will be invited for dinner."

As suggested by him, both descended a number of steps leading to the sacred river in which they bathed and also washed their clothes. Coming up to the temple courtyard, they spread the wet clothes in the sun for drying and sat there warming themselves from the same source of heat. The following thoughts then crossed Ramdas' mind:

"O Ram, Thou hast brought Thy unworthy slave to this temple because of the greatness of the saint Sri Ramakrishna, who flourished here at one time and whose teachings have spread all over the world. Somehow, Thou hast prevented Thy slave from leaving the place in the morning. After the midday meal he has to bid farewell to the place. But before doing so, would it not be well, O Ram, to acquaint Thy slave with the spot where the great saint lived and performed his austerities and meditation?"

Scarcely five minutes had passed since these thoughts were working in his mind, when a young and tall *sannyasi* dressed in a coat reaching nearly to his feet, and his forehead smeared with stripes of *chandan*, i.e., sandal paste[4], walked up to where Ramdas was sitting, and sat beside him. After an exchange of salutes, he spoke:

---

[4] *sandal paste*: made from wood of fragrant sandalwood tree

"Brother, have you not heard of the great saint of Dakshineshwar, Sri Ramakrishna Paramahamsa, who lived here some years ago?"

"Yes friend, Ram has brought his *das* here for that very reason," replied Ramdas who was then wondering at the inscrutable ways of Ram.

"Well then," said the Bengali sadhu, (for he was a Bengali), "Come along with me. I shall show you all the places connected with his life here."

O Ram, in what words shall Thy poor untutored slave measure the depths of the fountain of Thy love for Thy *das*? No sooner does he speak out his wish than it is fulfilled! The Bengali sadhu led the humble Ramdas (the sadhu–Ram did not accompany him) into a room forming a part of the rows of buildings that surrounded the square yard of the temple. The room was locked! The kind sadhu called for the key and opening the door, let in Ramdas. Oh, the joy of it all! Inside was found a cot on which there were a bed and two cushions used by Sri Ramakrishna, preserved in his memory. Ramdas, approaching them reverently, laid his head on them by turns. By this time he was beginning to feel the electric influence of the very air inside that room. Thrill after thrill of joy passed through him. He then laid himself flat on the floor of the room and began to roll all over the place, feeling all the while an inexpressible ecstasy of bliss. O Ram, the floor was blessed by the tread of the sacred feet of that holy man. About half an hour passed thus and he was still rolling on the floor, his face beaming with a strange light of infinite joy.

17.

Taraknath Temple

THE BENGALI SADHU was standing simply staring at the spectacle. At last, coming to himself, he suggested they might go out of the room, as other spots had also to be visited. Most reluctantly, Ramdas got up and came out of that heavenly place. Next, the sadhu guided him—and he was in a state of complete dreaminess at the time—to a garden behind the room, and pointed to a cluster of five trees called *panchavati*[1], around which a circular platform of earth and stones was raised.

"Here, the Paramahamsa used to sit frequently and offer *upadesh* to his disciples," explained the sadhu.

Then he led the way to a small hut wherein, he said, the saint used to sit in *samadhi* or deep meditation of his favorite ideal—Mother Kali. O Ramdas, thy eyes are indeed blessed by these sights—flow on tears, warm with the glow of supreme happiness.

Now, the Bengali sadhu proposed to take him on a visit to a young *sannyasi*—a disciple of Sri Ramakrishna. Agreeing, he was escorted and led away from the temple site for about a mile, where two *sannyasis* were found busy worshipping in front of the pictures of the Paramahamsa and Kali, placed in a small *mandir*[2]. Ramdas and the sadhu, on prostrating before

---

[1] *panchavati*: a grove of five sacred trees used by Sri Ramakrishna for his spiritual practices
[2] *mandir*: Hindu temple

the *sannyasis*, were invited to sit inside the temple. The *puja* over, they were given some *prasad*, on partaking of which they sought permission to depart. Coming back to the Kali temple, the Bengali *sannyasi* led the two sadhus to the banks of the Ganges where the steamboat jetty was situated. From this place the *sannyasi* pointed out the place called Belur Math, on the other side of the Ganges. He procured tickets for Ramdas and the sadhu–Ram and conducted them to the steamboat, which they duly boarded. But before leaving, he suggested that when travelling onwards by rail they might make a halt at a shrine called Taraknath or Tarakeshwar, a place worth visiting. This suggestion was kept in mind since it came from Ram Himself, whose kindness was felt at every step of this most marvelous and memorable pilgrimage.

In due course both the sadhus landed on the opposite side of the Ganges. A walk of about two furlongs brought them to a small temple where there resided a number of young men belonging to different parts of India. One of them took the sadhus inside the temple, in which a painting of the Paramahamsa was placed for daily worship. On enquiry, it was found that the temple was erected over the ashes of Sri Ramakrishna. Then the sadhus visited the beautiful *samadhis*[3] raised over the remains of Swami Vivekananda and the Holy Mother (wife of Sri Ramakrishna). Ramdas, wishing to spend a night at the Math, expressed his desire to the friends of the place, but was told that as there was no accommodation it was not possible to accede to his request. It was all the wish of Ram who does everything for good.

Thence they proceeded to the nearest railway station and got into a train going west, and one morning they found themselves at the Tarakeshwar station where they alighted. They proceeded straight to the famous temple of Taraknath, in which it is said a *Shiva–ling*[4] had its spontaneous birth breaking up the roots of a palmyrah tree—hence the name Taraknath.

---
[3] *samadhis*: here, tombs of saints
[4] *Shiva–ling*: symbol of Lord Shiva

After a bath and *darshan*, the sadhus went out to the city. Making enquiries, they learnt that some liberal Rajah was feeding 40 to 50 sadhus every day with a sumptuous dinner. Coming to the place they waited, along with many others, outside the *dharmashala*.

About 11 o'clock, an old friend, the manager of the *kshetra*[5], called in the sadhus counting the number required, and let them in, one by one. On a long veranda, in two rows facing each other, all the sadhus sat down and leafy plates were placed before them. When the food was being served, a new sadhu of middle age came in and demanded food. The manager of the *kshetra* at first refused to take him as the number to be fed was complete. But at the mention of the fact by the sadhu that he had not had meals for two days past, he was also offered a leaf and he sat down at a place which happened to be just opposite to Ramdas. The dinner consisted of wheat *puris* pretty thick and about sixteen inches in diameter, some *bhaji* or curry, and sweets. At first, each was served with two *puris* and sweets, etc. The *puris* having been prepared out of mill-made mixed wheat flour, were flexible like rubber. Ramdas was wanting in teeth—in all he had not half a dozen in his mouth. Even those who had the full complement had to struggle hard with the *puris* before they could be thrust down the throat. Ramdas' case was hence unique.

Now the sadhu, the latest arrival for the dinner, sitting in front, was observed to have finished his share in less than two minutes. He was served again with four *puris* which also disappeared in a trice. Again four more, and they met with the same fate! The sadhu was looking up for more! At this juncture, the old friend ordered the cook to fetch out the whole stock of *puris* from the kitchen. Then he approached the sadhu and said:

"Maharaj, you may take as many as you like," and he served one, two, three, four and so on and on until he counted twenty.

---

[5] *kshetra*: feeding center

Still the sadhu would not stop. Four more and the friend stopped, assuring the sadhu that he shall have some more after finishing those already served. At this stage, the attention of all sadhus was directed towards this voracious eater. All commenced to watch his eating process. But for himself the sadhu was calm and determined. *Puri* after *puri* disappeared. It mattered not for him what was going on around him. At every four or five *puris* he was drinking water out of a big brass pot he had by his side. Most of the sadhus present there could not eat more than four each. The record with some did not exceed six *puris*. But the phenomenal sadhu had been served in all 34 *puris*. He was also served more *bhaji* or curry and sweets. He ate them all, with one potful of water into the bargain.

The affair is narrated here, not out of any disrespect to the sadhu, but to apprise the reader of the case of a man who had a tremendous appetite, showing forth the wonderful *maya*[6] of Ram.

After two days' stay at the shrine, Ramdas and the sadhu–Ram left the station and came to Gaya, where they obtained *darshan* in the temple and had a bath in the holy river Phalguni. The next day they started, and reached the famous shrine of the North—Kashi.

---

[6] *maya*: illusion

18.

KASHI

THE CITY OF KASHI[1] is a city of magnificent temples, the domes and turrets of which, when viewed from a height, lend a charm to the scene on the banks of the holy river Ganges. The whole of India rightly recognizes that Kashi is one of the most important shrines of Hindustan. Every day, pilgrims by thousands are pouring into the place from all parts of India. As Ram took Ramdas on this pilgrimage in winter, the cold was very great here, and the sadhu–Ram and he had not sufficient clothing, and sleeping as they were in an open place on the bank of the river, the cold was felt very acutely—especially by the sadhu–Ram. The sadhu–Ram was getting impatient every day. His main object of travelling in the North seemed to have been fulfilled after visiting Kashi. Now he wanted to return to South India. Ram's will. Nothing happens in this world but subject to His divine will. Ram's ways are inscrutable.

Next day, the train carried the sadhu–Ram and Ramdas to Ayodhya—the place where Sri Ramachandra lived and reigned. It was night when the pilgrims reached the place. They rested for the night in the open passenger shed outside the station. The cold was intense. The sadhu–Ram suggested that both should lie down back to back, the backs touching each other. This device was adopted in order to exchange one

---
[1] Benares

another's heat of the body for mutual warmth. Really an original idea! Thus passed the night. Early next day, both proceeded to the city and then to the Sarayu River. Washing the hands and feet, the sadhu-Ram suggested that no bath need be taken as the cold was very great. So, returning from the holy river, they visited various *mandirs* of Sri Ramachandra and Hanumanji, secured food at a *kshetra* and that very night caught a train going down towards Bombay.

Now, the sadhu-Ram had once and for all decided to close the northern India pilgrimage and hence the journey towards Bombay. O Ram, Thy will is supreme. Although Ramdas has yet to visit more shrines of North India, it is beyond Thy humble slave to know the reason for Thy taking him to Bombay. Every move Thou givest to the situation of Thy *das* is considered by him to be for the best. The train travelled taking the sadhus south and south. Station after station was passed. At a small station, while the sadhu-Ram was dozing, some passenger who had not perhaps any pot with him, took away, while alighting, the brass pot of the sadhu-Ram, who woke up and discovered his loss after the train had left that station. He began to fret over the loss a great deal—in fact he wept bitterly over it like a child.

The next station was Jhansi which was duly reached. Here the ticket inspection was very strict. So the ticket clerk pulled down these sadhus as well as many others from other carriages, and led them all near the gate leading out of the station. There were in all about ten sadhus. The ticket clerk made all of them stand in a line on one side of the entrance or exit. It was both. The passengers were now going out of the station and the clerk was collecting tickets at the gate, his back turned against the sadhus, who were made to stand only at arm's length from the clerk. The first in the line of the sadhus was a young *sannyasi* with a *jatah* or tuft of matted hair. Whenever the ticket clerk had a momentary respite from the collection of tickets, he would turn round and clutching the *jatah* of the young sadhu, who was nearest to him, shake his head violently.

The next moment he had to attend to ticket collection. When the stream of passengers thinned and there was some break, he would again handle the head of the sadhu and give it a shake or inflict blows upon it with his fist. While this was going on, by a look at the face of the sadhu, who was next to him in the line, Ramdas made out that there was a happy smile on the face of the young sadhu.

19.

Love Conquers Hate

THE SADHU SEEMED TO ENJOY the treatment. He was calm and contented. Ramdas, wishing also to taste the pleasure, requested the sadhu to exchange places with him and thus offer him also the unique opportunity of receiving the attention of the ticket clerk. But the sadhu would not be persuaded to abandon his enviable position. Off and on, the clerk was meting out this treatment to the willing sadhu. This continued for nearly half an hour. The ticket collection work at last stopped. Now the clerk was totally free from work, and he turned right towards the sadhus. He approached the other sadhus, of whom Ramdas was the second, with the object of handling them roughly one by one. Ramdas felt much relieved to see that his turn had at last come. The clerk coming up, caught his hand in a firm grasp and looked on his face in which he discovered a most welcome smile, bright and beaming. At once he let go his hand and drawing himself back a few steps seemed to have given himself to some thinking. It was Ram who was at work. For, next instant, he asked all the sadhus to go out of the station. Accordingly all the sadhus left the station and went out one by one.

O Ram! When Thy invincible arm protects Thy slave where was fear for him? One thing was proved incontestably and beyond any doubt and that was—Thou disarmest the evil intentions of an adversary when he approaches you in a violent mood by meeting him with a smile instead of with fear or hatred. Love can surely conquer hate. Love is a sovereign antidote for all the ills of the world. After all, the whole occurrence might be only Ram testing the sadhus to see if they would lose their self-control under provocation. All that Ram does is for the best.

Now the time was about 2 o'clock past midnight. It was pitch dark. So the sadhus sought for a place on the station for taking rest for the night. But conditions for this were far from favorable. The station was full to overflowing, as it were, with passengers. Every available nook and corner of that portion of the station intended for passengers was occupied, and they were all scattered on the floor, sleeping in fantastic postures—all space filled up. However, Ramdas and his guide, the sadhu-Ram, crept near a pillar where there was found room for both to sit on their legs. The cold here also was very severe. The sadhus sat up close to and pressing each other, so much so, that they seemed almost molded into one piece. *Ram-bhajan* was going on. Ramdas became unconscious and dozed away where he sat and did not wake up until he was roused by a strong and shrill voice asking all passengers to take to their feet and walk out of the station. This was the order of the railway police.

Ramdas opened his eyes and instantly became conscious of his body which was discovered to be in a peculiar condition—the legs had turned so stiff with cold that they had stuck fast at the bend of the knee joint, and on a look at them he further made out that from the knee downwards both the legs had swollen, and also the feet, as though they were stricken with elephantiasis. However by rubbing them briskly by both hands for about five minutes, he could unlock the stiffened joints. Slowly rising up, he hobbled along for some distance. As he walked on, the stiffness disappeared. About 8 a.m. they reached the city of Jhansi—about four miles from the station.

20.

JHANSI

MAKING ENQUIRIES, they straightaway went to a *dharmashala* and, resting here for some time, at the suggestion of the sadhu–Ram, directed their steps to the bazaar and obtaining some flour, etc., from a charitable merchant, the sadhu–Ram prepared a few *rotis* and *dal* curry[1]. After finishing dinner they remained in the *dharmashala* till evening. Then the sadhu–Ram proposed a move towards the station which was reached before dark. The same ticket clerk, whom Ram had brought them in touch with the previous night, was found at the gate. Ramdas went to him and requested him to allow them to proceed to Bombay by the night train. Although at first he consented to do so, when the train arrived at 2 a.m. he refused them admission to the platform. It was all Ram's wish. So they had to spend another night in the station, which meant cold, stiffening and swelling of the limbs for a second time.

Next morning, they retraced their steps again to the city. The state of the sadhu–Ram's mind at this time was most miserable. Coming to the same *dharmashala*, they met two Telugu sadhus. The sadhu–Ram, after a short talk with these sadhus, at once made up his mind to give up the company of Ramdas and join them. It was again all Ram's making. His ways are always inscrutable. Total submission to Him means no anxiety, no fear, no pain, and all assurance. About half an hour later

---
[1] *dal curry*: pureed lentils

Ramdas was left alone in the company of Ram whose name he was uttering without cessation. The new sadhus and the sadhu-Ram—who was so long his guide and foster-mother, as it were—departed from the *dharmashala*. Ramdas was meditating on Ram unconcerned at the severance of the sadhu-Ram's company; for complete resignation to the will of Ram had deprived him of all sense of anxiety and cares for the future. Thus, time was passing in *Ram-bhajan* when two friends coming up to him dropped into his hands two one *anna* pieces, suggesting that he might purchase some eatables from the bazaar and break his fast. Accordingly, he directed his steps to the bazaar. Here, while purchasing some eatables from a sweetmeat shop, he felt at his elbow somebody pulling him. He had now received the eatables. Turning around he heard the friend address him:

"Maharaj, a *seth*[2] desires you to go over to him."

Ramdas instantly followed the friend who led him into a shop, wherein were piled up wheat bags. As he entered the place, a friend came up from inside the shop and fell prostrate at the feet of Ramdas—the mendicant. Rising up with folded hands, the friend requested him to accept *bhiksha* at his house that day. This friend was the merchant who had sent for him. He was then asked to sit on a thick white mattress—called *gadi*—with cushions to lean against. But Ramdas was a humble slave of Ram. So he preferred to sit on the floor. Here again he was offered a gunny bag on which he sat. After dinner the kind-hearted merchant sat beside him and put him some questions in regard to his movements, etc.—which were all duly answered in terms of Ram's will, which was alone his sole guide. He further told the *seth* of Ram's kindness and love for his *bhaktas* and how he who trusts Ram knows no sorrow and can be happy under all circumstances.

To have Ram's name on the lips means joy—pure joy—nothing but joy. The merchant was visibly affected to hear

---

[2] *seth*: merchant

these words for he was himself a great *Ramabhakta*[3]. "Sitaram, Sitaram,"[4] was always on his tongue. After a few minutes' talk, the *seth* entreated Ramdas to remain with him for some days. He said that Ramdas' body, which was then in a most neglected condition, required to be taken care of and that Ram had especially sent Ramdas to him with this sole object. It must be related here that the clothes in which he was clad were all rags. Mahadev Prasad—such was the name of the merchant in whose care he was placed by Ram—provided him with new clothes dyed in *gerrua*, and every care was taken of him by this kind host. Mahadev became extremely fond of him. At nights, in spite of remonstrances Mahadev Prasad would sit beside the sleeping Ramdas and press his feet. O, the kindness he showered on poor and humble Ramdas was unbounded. O Ram, it was Thee who was doing it all through that friend. O Ram, how good, how loving Thou art! Weep on—weep on Ramdas—in silence, weep on—weep not in sorrow but in joy, because Ram's grace is upon you.

For a month he was detained by Mahadev with him. Throughout the day and night he would not give up the company of Ramdas. At his request Ramdas was explaining to him the meaning of some *slokas* from the *Bhagavad Gita* with the help of the small understanding with which he was gifted by Ram, and Mahadev in return would read out and explain that monumental work of Tulsidas—the Hindi *Ramayan*[5]. All people in his house were also very hospitable and kind to Ramdas. To prevent any cold affecting the heart of frail-bodied Ramdas, Mahadev got a tight woolen jacket made for him. O Ram, how kind of Thee! When Thou art out to show Thy fondness and love for Thy slave, Thou shameth the very human mother who gave birth to Ramdas' body. Such is Thy unlimited love.

---
[3] *Ramabhakta*: one who is devoted to God
[4] *Sitaram*: Mystical union of the manifest and unmanifest aspects of God. Sita is Divine Mother incarnated as Rama's consort and queen
[5] *Ramayana*: Hindu epic, the story of Rama and Sita

During Ramdas' stay at Jhansi, Mahadev Prasad took him on a visit to two Mohammedan saints. The first was an aged saint named Mirzaji. He might have been over 60 years of age, lean and bent. He would not speak, but there was a cheerful twinkle in his eyes. In short, he was a mere baby—simple, innocent and free. Mahadev Prasad had brought some eatables with him which he thrust into the saint's mouth bit by bit. There was not a single tooth in the saint's mouth. The eatables were soft sweets. He chewed and swallowed them unconcernedly. He seemed to recognize nobody. His eyes had an absent and vacant look, though bright. He was visited twice. On the second occasion, he was found sitting on the ground outside his cottage, quietly tearing to bits stray pieces of paper scattered around him.

21.

MEDITATION THE ONLY WAY

THE OTHER SAINT whose name was Pirjee was comparatively a younger man than Mirzaji. He would speak and reply to questions put to him. Mahadev asked Pirjee whether happiness could be found in the *samsaric* life in which he was placed. At his question, Pirjee seemed to have roused himself a little. His voice was firm and decisive.

"Well brother, as I have told you several times, there is only one remedy and that is, give up, give up the miserable life of the world and going up to a solitary place, meditate upon God who alone can give you the happiness you are after. This is the only way and no other."

O Ram, Thou hast brought Thy slave in touch with these saints in order to confirm his faith in Thee. The first saint teaches the state of one who reached Thee. The second teaches how to reach Thee.

The kind Mahadev was taking him in the nights to various *bhajan* parties in the city. When Ramdas told him one day that it seemed to be Ram's wish that he should make a move, he was quite unwilling to part from Ramdas. To avoid an immediate contingency of a departure, he escorted him to a village called Oorcha which was about six miles from the city. The place is famous for the temple of Sri Ramachandra. Leaving him at this place, and after arranging for his food with a mother living near the temple, Mahadev Prasad returned to the city. His parting words were:

"You may remain here as long as you like or as long as Ram wishes you to remain. When He desires you to leave the place, kindly come back to me at Jhansi."

When left alone in contemplation of the Divine Guide, Protector and Mother Ram, Ramdas wandered on the bank of the beautiful river of the place. On walking for about two miles he came upon a number of *samadhis* or tombs—some very old and dilapidated, over which were erected tall conical turrets that shot high up into the air. He understood, on enquiry in the village later, that they were the graves of women who performed *sati*[1]—a custom prevailing in olden days. This place is now used as a cremation ground. The site is full of trees and a beautiful calm reigns over the place. He decided—as prompted by Ram—to occupy one of the tombs for a retreat. For eight days he remained at this place. Only for about an hour at midday he would go to the temple and receive the rations prepared by the old mother, which consisted of a few saltless *rotis* and boiled potatoes.

The whole night he would sit up for *Ram-bhajan* in that tomb. Nights were spent in ecstasy. Ram's presence was felt in the very air he was breathing. In the mornings when he was repeating aloud the charming *mantram*—"Om Sri Ram Jai Ram Jai Jai Ram!" the birds of the air, small and big, and squirrels would alight on the parapet wall and would listen eagerly and with rapt attention to the sound of the great *pranava*—Om! In the evening the same sound "Om" would work like magic upon the goats and bullocks that came near the tomb for grazing. They would raise their heads pricking up their ears, stand still and drink in the sound. O Ram, it is proved beyond any doubt that Thou resideth in the hearts of all creatures. The sleeping souls of the birds of the air and the beasts of the plains are awakened at the call of Ram's glorious voice!

---

[1]*sati*: self-immolation of a wife on the funeral pyre of husband

22.

RAM, THE FRIEND OF THE POOR

DURING HIS VISITS to the village, the villagers tried to dissuade Ramdas from staying in that jungle at nights as they warned him of tigers and other wild animals, because the place occupied by him formed part of a dense and extensive forest. But when the all-powerful Ram was there to save him, where was fear for him and from whom? Ram is pervading everywhere—in all things, in all beings, in all creatures. He continued there for eight days, when he received the command from Ram to move on.

A small incident which took place here has to be chronicled at this stage. One day, when he was passing the small bazaar of this place with his *lota* in hand, he felt thirsty. He now approached, as he walked on, a number of small low huts on one side of the road. Going up to one of them, at its entrance he found an old mother sitting. He begged of her to give him some water in his *lota*. The old mother shook her head and said: "Maharaj, you cannot take water at my hands."

"May Ramdas know the reason for this objection?" inquired Ramdas.

"The simple reason is," put in the mother, "I belong to a very low caste. To be brief, I am a barber woman."

"What of that?" said Ramdas, nothing surprised. "You are Ramdas' mother all the same—kindly satisfy the thirst of your son."

She was highly pleased at this reply, and going in brought out a seat for him and her water vessel out of which she poured some water into his *lota*. He quenched his thirst occupying the seat so kindly offered by her. Now the old mother said that she was utterly miserable. Left alone in the world, she spent all her days and nights in pain, fear and anxiety. Ramdas then assured her:

"O mother, there is no cause for fear and anxiety or for a feeling of loneliness when there is Ram to protect us all—Ram is always near us."

"But a poor, weak-minded woman like myself does not possess any faith in Ram, because I am a sinner." So saying the mother burst into tears.

"You shall have faith, kind mother, by the grace of Ram. Don't despair, Ram is always the friend of the poor and the humble," said Ramdas.

"Then show me the way," asked the old mother.

"Repeat the one name 'Ram' at all times of the day and at nights when you are awake. You may be sure that you will not feel lonely or miserable as long as you are uttering that glorious name. Where this name is sounded or meditated upon there resides no sorrow, no anxiety—nay, not even death."

Saying thus, Ramdas started to go, when she begged him to visit her again the next day. As desired by her, he went to her hut again the following day at about the same time.

"Well mother, how do you do?" was his question.

There was a cheerful smile on the face of the mother. She said that she had acted upon his advice and was finding herself much relieved from fear and cares. Then she offered him some *ladoos*[1] which she said she had got from the sweet-meat shop.

"Mother, this is not what Ramdas wants, he wants something prepared by your own hands," said he.

At this she went in and got for him, a piece of *roti* or bread made by her which he ate with no small amount of pleasure. Later, he saw her once again, when she was busy uttering "Ram, Ram!"

---

[1] *ladoo*: a kind of sweet confection

23.

God Never Punishes

By Ram's command Ramdas came back to Jhansi, where Mahadev Prasad welcomed him most heartily and pressed him to spend a few more days with him. At this time Ram brought him into contact with more than a dozen friends at Jhansi, who were all very kind and hospitable to him. Of these, one young friend named Ramkinker was extremely kind. One day, in the course of a conversation, he heard that on the Himalayas there were two shrines—Kedarnath and Badrinath—and the path leading to these places was very difficult, and also the cold there was very intense. O Ram, it was all your suggestion. For him there was always a fascination for dangerous journeys and perilous places. Kedarnath—he had read of in the splendid writings of that great *Mahatma*—Swami Rama Tirtha. His mind was made up. Ram prompted and the resolution was sealed that he should visit these shrines, however difficult the path that led to them. He expressed Ram's wish to his friends. Mahadev and others who valued his frail body so dearly, did not at first appreciate the idea. They said that the journey was a terrible one and it would prove so especially to Ramdas whose body was so weak and emaciated. He replied:

"Ram has given his fiat and Ramdas obeys, placing full trust in Him. The burden is on Ram to see that he is taken care of; even if his body were to drop off at the will of Ram, he would not grumble. He will then be Ram's entirely—go he must."

At once Ramkinker, the young friend, proposed to follow him on his journey to Kedarnath and Badrinath. So he had to remain at Jhansi for some days more at the request of these friends, which gave Ramkinker sufficient time to make his preparations for the journey.

Some other incidents in connection with his stay at Jhansi have to be narrated here before he describes his pilgrimage to the Himalayas. After the resolution was made, he was taken over by Ramkinker, who kept him in a *Rammandir* near his own house and carefully looked after his personal wants. In this *mandir* there was a *pujari*—known as Pandaji—O Pandaji! How very kind you were too. At midday, every day, Ramdas would saunter out in the hot sun and walk in the streets of Jhansi for two or three hours. The heat of the sun at midday in that season was very severe, but he would not mind it. Observing this one day, Pandaji, who was treating him like a child, warned him thus:

"Look here, Maharaj, you are every day going out at midday and wandering about in the hot sun. Your head, which is clean-shaven, is always uncovered. If you are obstinate, I shall have to lock you up in the temple before I go out."

With this threat—an indication of his great love for Ramdas—he would press him to sleep in the afternoon and would not leave the *mandir* for midday meals until he saw Ramdas asleep. O Ram, how kind Thou art!

One day, during his midday walks, Ramdas got thirsty and he discovered on the way a well at which some mothers were drawing water. He went up to the place and requested one of them to give him some water to quench his thirst. In reply, the mother who was asked for water said:

"Maharaj, I am a Mohammedan and you being a Hindu monk, it is not proper that you should accept water at my hands."

"O mother!" replied he, "Ramdas knows no caste distinctions. He finds in you that Universal Mother, Sita, as he finds in all women. Therefore, do not hesitate to provide your son with some water."

The mother was strangely surprised at this reply, washed the water pot thoroughly, and drawing water afresh, poured it out in the hollow of his hands, and he drank as much water as he wanted. Then he continued his walk.

For about ten days he was staying in the *Rammandir*, and during evenings a number of friends of the city would come and put him various questions about Ram, and he would try to satisfy them by such replies as were prompted him by Ram Himself. On one occasion a certain friend came up specially to have a discussion with him on a religious point.

His first question was: "Who are you?"

"I am Ramdas," was his simple reply.

"No, you speak a lie there," retorted the friend. "You are Ram Himself. When you declare you are Ramdas, you do not know what you say. God is everywhere and in everything. He is in you and so you are He. Confess it right away."

"True, dear friend, God is everywhere," replied Ramdas. "But at the same time, it must be noted that God is one, and when He is in you and everywhere around you, may I humbly ask to whom you are putting this question?"

After reflecting for a time, the friend was driven to say: "Well, I have put the question to myself."

This reply was given as a desperate attempt to reconcile his first contention. If he would say that the question was put to Ramdas there was a clear sense of duality accepted by the disputant himself—"I and you."

"As a matter of fact," put in Ramdas, "Ram does not speak—the moment he speaks he is not Ram. Speech creates always a sense of duality—the speaker and the man spoken to. Ram is one and indivisible. It is sheer ignorance for a man whose ego is a great obstruction for his complete realization of the oneness of God—to say that he is God."

The friend persisted for some time more to uphold his argument and eventually gave it up. At the desire of Ramdas, who liked to stay for some days in a retired place, the friends at Jhansi took him to a garden about a mile away from the city, where there was a small shed. Here he lived for some days, visited every evening by a number of friends.

Here again a schoolmaster came for a discussion. He belonged to the Arya Samaj started by that great saint, Swami Dayananda Saraswati. This friend, in the course of a talk, became very hot and excited. The point was about the *shuddhi* movement[1] set on foot by Swami Shraddhanandji. Ramdas was clearly opposed to this movement as he is, in fact, opposed to every effort on the part of anybody to create differences in religious faiths. That all faiths lead to the same goal is a most beautiful and convincing truth. At the close of the discussion, the friend exceeded the limits of decent talk. However, Ramdas was cool and collected by the grace of Ram. At parting, he assured the friend that he loved him most dearly in spite of any objectionable words used by him. Next day, about the same time, this friend came again in a great hurry. He could scarcely talk. He could only whisper; his throat was choked up. His condition was pitiable.

"O Maharaj," he exclaimed, falling at the feet of Ramdas, "God has punished your slave for having used rough words to you yesterday. See how my throat is choked and I can't speak out properly."

"O friend, Ramdas is really sorry to hear this, but be assured of this—God never punishes. God is love and is always kind. Our own doubts are our enemies and create a lot of mischief. The so-called evil is of our own making."

At once, pulling out Ramdas' right hand the friend rubbed the palm on his throat and, strange to say, his throat cleared and he began to talk more clearly and in a few minutes he was all right!

"Behold! Maharaj, how powerful you are!" he cried exultantly.

"You make a mistake, dear friend," replied Ramdas. "Ramdas is a poor slave of Ram, possessing no powers at all. Your faith alone has cured you and nothing else."

---

[1] *shuddhi movement*: promoted reconversion to Hinduism

From this time onwards the friend became very much attached to him and was very kind. O Ram, Thy ways are so wonderful that Ramdas gets utterly bewildered at times.

The friends at Jhansi whom he met daily in that city were all very charitable in disposition—especially were they kind and hospitable to sadhus. When he was living with Mahadev Prasad, he found this friend a pattern of charity and humility. Mahadev would never send away a hungry man from his door without feeding him. He would forego his own meal to satisfy a hungry man. His heart was so soft and so tender. Mahadev's humility was exemplary. Ram certainly gave Ramdas the society of this friend so that he might know what true charity and humility meant in actual practice. Ramkinker—the young friend who accompanied him on his pilgrimage to the Himalayas—made it a rule to utilize about ten percent of his salary for charity. This is really a beautiful hint for all. While speaking of charity, the ideal of charity followed by the householder of northern India is indeed very noble and lofty, the ideal of the ancients, viz., that the householder has no right to exist as such if he does not share his food every day with a hungry man of no means, such as a beggar or a sadhu. In fact, it is declared that a man assumes *grihasthashrama*[2] with the specific object of carrying out this noble ideal. There are found some *grihasthas*[3] who would not wait for a guest to turn up but would go seeking for one in the streets, in temples or *dharmashalas*, such is the piety of the householders. Ramdas' experience in southern India was also full of incidents in which charity played a most laudable part. In fact, the whole of India is a great land of charity.

---

[2] *grihasthashrama*: the householder's life
[3] *grihasthas*: householders

24.

Himalayan Journey

THE FRIENDS IN JHANSI provided Ramdas with all the necessaries for the journey to the Himalayas, and the day for departure came. Many came as far as the railway station to bid farewell to humble Ramdas and Ramkinker. Both parties parted after mutual exchange of good wishes. In due time Hardwar was reached. Hardwar, as the name suggests, is the gateway to the great shrines of the Himalayas. Here the pilgrims stayed for two days. It is most delightful to visit the bank of the Ganga, where congregate *sannyasins, sannyasinis*[1], sadhus, *bhaktas, brahmins,* pious mothers—all busy with baths, ablutions, *sandhya,* prayers and worship. O Ram, Thou art clearly manifest at this holy place!

Now the journey on the Himalayas commenced. Up and up, Ramdas and Ramkinker mounted and reached the place called Rishikesh. Rishikesh is a very beautiful place. The scenes on the banks of the holy Ganga[2] are simply charming. Here the lofty peaks of mountains are dimly visible at a distance, covered over with white mist, kissing as they do the rolling waves of clouds that hang above them. A nearer gaze presents to the eye high gigantic rocks with dense forests, a mixture of green, yellow and red hues of leaves, foliage and blossoms. A still nearer view shows the crystal water of the

---

[1] *sannyasini*: woman sannyasin or renunciant
[2] *Ganga*: the holy river Ganges

holy Ganga that flows in all calmness and majesty, disclosing in her bosom huge pieces of rocks which her rushing torrent had pulled down in days of yore, and made round and smooth. O Ram, Thou art sublime!

On one side of the great river are seen a number of small thatched huts, neat and clean—*ashrams* of *sannyasis*. Ramkinker took Ramdas into one of these huts. The interior of the hut was fitted with the simplest furniture. A bamboo cot, two posts of which form the pillars of the hut itself, on which was spread a deer-skin and a *kambal* or blanket lying in folds at the foot of it. A venerable old *sannyasi* was squatting upon the deer-skin. On a peg was hanging his *kamandal*[3] made of a black shell. Except a small piece of cloth and a spare *kaupin*[4] which were drying in the sun outside, he had no other clothing. On the sandy floor of the hut was a bamboo-mat, and in a corner were two black stones, one big and the other small, for crushing almonds and such other hard eatables having shells to break. There was a calm and peaceful look upon the countenance of the saint. He welcomed Ramkinker and Ramdas with a cheerful smile, and they seated themselves on the mat after prostrating at the feet of the *mahatma*. He offered some cardamoms to the guests and had a simple and childlike talk with them about saints who would be found in the thick forests on the opposite bank of the Ganges, unexplored by ordinary man, where for a number of years they might be performing *tapasya*[5].

His beautiful advice to Ramdas was to remain as long as possible for his *sadhana*[6] in solitude, than which there is no better means for control of the mind. He was kind, affable, engaging and good. O Ram, it was Thyself in all Thy glory that Ramdas met under that simple roof. One thing more, this saint was very fond of birds. He would not miss to share his food with them every day. They would wait for their share on the

---

[3] *kamandal*: water vessel
[4] *kaupin*: loin cloth
[5] *tapasya*: austerities
[6] *sadhana*: spiritual practices

trees outside the hut. He talked very lovingly of them. After coming out, Ramkinker and Ramdas wandered on the bank of Mother Ganga, where they saw a number of *sannyasis* clad in orange robes, their faces beaming with a cheerful light. They had all come out for their usual morning bath in the holy waters. Ramdas, during his stay in Rishikesh, had occupied the mud-platform around a banyan tree on the bank of the river close to the hut of a *mahatma*. This saint was also very kind to Ramdas. His hobby was to feed cows and monkeys, who would always be crowding round his hut. In order to feed them he would go a-begging in the bazaar and secure foodstuffs and grass. He was finding a peculiar pleasure in childishly dancing with monkeys, running after them, making strange noises, all in glee and sport. His face was bright, and his greenish eyes would twinkle always with a watery tenderness. Under the same tree there was also a blind sadhu who had a good voice, which he made a right use of by singing the glory of Ram.

Three days were spent here in all peace and happiness. Ramkinker was kind enough to attend to Ramdas' food. There are two big *annakshetras*[7] in Rishikesh which daily furnish food to all the *sannyasis*. Of these *kshetras*, one was started by a great *mahatma* by the name of Kalikambli Baba who is now in *mahasamadhi*[8]. On these mountains and among sadhus his blessed name is on the lips of all. With his influence he has induced the wealthy merchants of Bombay and other places to open, at every ten or fifteen miles on the hills, a *dharmashala* in which *sadavart* or food-stuffs are distributed free to all sadhu-pilgrims who hold chits with which they are provided at Rishikesh. Ramkinker secured these chits for Ramdas at Rishikesh.

---

[7] *annakshetra*: kitchen offering free food to pilgrims
[8] *mahasamadhi*: literally absorption in God, term for death of saint

25.

HIMALAYAN JOURNEY (CONTINUED)

ON THE FOURTH DAY, they started on their journey higher on the hills. As they climbed higher and higher, the scenes and landscapes they saw were found to be simply enchanting. On the right the sacred Ganga was rushing downhill in all her glory, and on the left, high rocky hills, full of foliage and trees, presented at once a thrilling and absorbing sight. The very air there was charged with the divine presence of Ram. The far-off hills and valleys, the varied-hued sky in which the white fleecy clouds assumed fantastic shapes, the snowcapped mountains, hundreds of miles away up, dazzling in the rays of the sun as though they were covered with sheets of silver—all these constituted indeed, an imposing sight! Oh, the charm of the scenes! O Ram! Poor Ramdas cannot find adequate words to describe the grandeur, the beauty, the wonderful glory of the sights that met his bewildering gaze.

As he walked on, he drank deeper and deeper of the splendor of Ram's infinity and was lost, lost, lost in the intoxication of it all. O Ram, Thy kindness to Thy slave is really unbounded. From day to day both Ramkinker and Ramdas walked on at a high speed. Ramdas felt no fatigue, no pain, no discomfort of any kind. He was as fresh as ever. It was all due to Ram's grace whose name was always on his lips. Thus mountain after mountain was traversed, and as they climbed on, grander and newer scenes presented themselves before their wondering sight. It was a journey in the land of enchantment.

It was all a bewitching dream full of the glory and greatness of Ram. There Ram exhibits His marvelous powers. He is a mighty conjurer, vision after vision dances and flits before your eyes, and unconsciously you fall under the subtle charm and spell of this great Magician. You forget what you are and where you are. You are simply absorbed and lost in the surroundings—like a wisp of smoke in a hurricane.

Ramdas was walking at high speed—nay, he was veritably flying. Even the difficult ascents were scaled in no time. Most of the time he was unconscious of his body. His mind was entirely merged in Ram, who alone appeared to him in those enchanting scenes. Higher and higher climbed the indefatigable pilgrims. Ramkinker, who had a heavy bundle to carry, complained of Ramdas' running speed, since he could not keep pace with him. But Ramdas was not his own master. Ram was his master. At a certain place they missed each other, causing anxiety to both; but, however, Ram brought them together at a stage called Rudraprayag. Thousands of pilgrims are every year ascending these hills and during this season, i.e., from March to June, a regular stream of people is going up and coming down the hills. All the pilgrims, sadhus and others whom Ramdas met on the way were very kind to him. Some rich merchants from cities like Bombay were very solicitous. Because Ram is kind, all are kind, and Ram is in all.

The mountains are peopled by hill tribes—a fair-complexioned and well-built race. They live by cultivation and cattle and goat breeding. Naturally their lives and ways are simple. Their faith in God is very great. "Ram, Ram," is always on their lips. If you talk to them they tell you with a glow of pride that they are the descendants of the *Rishis*[1] that lived in those hills. Their clothing is wholly made of wool. Males wear long woolen coats and drawers and a black cap, and women, rough blankets in place of *saris*[2]. These blankets are prepared there out of the wool yielded by the sheep they tend. So the foodstuffs and

---
[1] *rishis*: sages of ancient India
[2] *sari*: traditional dress worn by Indian women

clothing—two essentials of life—are the produce of their own labor. Even while walking from place to place, every man and woman carries a quantity of wool which he or she is spinning on the way. They have simple pit looms on which they weave the yarn into cloth. Since their mode of life is free from the baneful touch of modern civilization, they live simple, pure, honest and pious lives.

At different stages of the journey over the hills, under trees or in small huts or caves, are seen sadhus engaged in austerities. To seek their company and remain there, for ever so small a period, is a great privilege. The society of a sadhu is a much needed bath for the mind. The pure atmosphere he creates around him by his meditations is the river in which the mind bathes and is purged of evil thoughts and impressions. Upon these sacred hills are the *ashramas* of such famous saints as Narada and Agastya Muni. There is also a place called Pandukeshar where the Pandavas[3] are said to have halted for some time during their journey to Kailas[4]. There is a temple here and some old inscriptions upon plates of copper. The first place visited by Ramdas and Ramkinker on the heights was Trijugnarain. The ascent to this spot was sharp and steep, and it was a plateau surrounded by hills covered with snow. Hence the cold here was intense. The pilgrims remained here for one day.

Then after descending some distance another chain of hills was mounted. Here the path was narrow, rugged and dangerous—frail, rickety bridges had to be crossed—at three places large tracts of snow had to be traversed. On account of the perilous nature of the path, every year many pilgrims are reported to have slipped down the cliffs and been washed away in the rushing torrents of the river, many hundreds of feet below. One instance of a narrow escape may be mentioned here.

At a certain stage in the middle of an ascent, Ramdas was sitting on the path awaiting Ramkinker. This was the edge of a high cliff and the river was flowing far below. The path was very nar-

---
[3] *Pandavas*: five hero brothers of the Indian epic, Mahabharata
[4] *Kailas*: a holy mountain in the Himalayas, regarded as the abode of Lord Shiva

row. A girl of about 16 years, full of energy and activity, was coming down on her return journey. It was a sharp descent. Her pace was rapid and the sharp downhill path only accelerated her speed, and in spite of herself she was running down at uncontrollable velocity. Down, down she came. She was excited, her face was flushed and she knew she was being drawn down automatically, and it was beyond her power to control herself. Instead of running towards the hill-side, she was staggering down to the edge of the path—the very brow of a precipice.

Ramdas watched the scene with breathless suspense. He was silently calling upon Ram to save her. Ram alone could and none else. Now she came up to the edge, and with a superhuman effort controlled herself. She had come to the very brink. Part of her left foot was out of the edge. O Ram, how terrible a condition! Ram, Thy name be glorified. Ramdas looks and sees the girl falling on the path right across uttering "Ram, Ram." Saved, saved! Ram saved her! She got up, did not wait a minute, but continued her walk further down. Dauntless girl! What a marvelous faith in Ram is thine!

The other was the case of an old woman who gave up her body in the basket in which she was being carried by a sturdy mountaineer who was specially engaged for the purpose. At certain stages in the journey this carrier would lower down his burden for relief, and the last time he did so, it happened to be near the place where Ramkinker and Ramdas were resting on the roadside. The bearer, as usual with him, lowered the basket on a rock and asked the old mother to step out of the basket for some time. But receiving no reply, the hillman peeped into the basket and a cry of surprise and pain started from him.

"The poor woman is gone," he exclaimed.

O Ram, Thy will is done. Then walking higher and higher, Ramdas and his kind guide eventually reached Kedarnath. This was indeed a grand place. It was plain land in the midst of high towering mountains covered with snow. The cold here was extremely severe. O Ram, Thy kindness to Thy slave was so great that Thou hadst made him almost proof against cold.

26.

HIMALAYAN JOURNEY (CONTINUED)

IN KEDARNATH Ramdas performed a most difficult feat—all by Ram's grace. He ascended one of the surrounding high rocks covered with snow. Of course, Ramkinker followed him. While going up they had to do so by holding the rough grass that grew on the hill. It was a steep ascent. For nearly half the way Ramkinker accompanied him, and then he refused to go higher up with Ramdas, both on account of cold and the danger of slipping down. Meanwhile Ramdas, who had surrendered himself into the hands of Ram, mounted higher and higher until he reached the summit of the hill and touched its narrow conical peak. As he touched the top he gave a cry of triumph in the name of Sri Ram. He uttered at the top of his voice: "Om Sri Ram Jai Ram Jai Jai Ram!" O Ram, what a glorious Being Thou art!

Now descent was most perilous, an unguarded step or a slight slip meant a headlong fall and certain destruction of the body. However, when Ram guides where is the fear? What danger cannot be faced boldly? He slowly crept down, nay, slipped down the hill. While doing so, it began to rain white solid globules of snow. He had ascended without any warm clothing. But by Ram's grace he felt neither cold nor fear. At last, Ram brought him safely to the base of the rock. It took five hours to accomplish this ascent; the height of the hill might have been over a mile. Going to the source of the River Mandakini, which starts at this place, where the snow melts and flows down, he took his bath. The water was, of course, very, very cold, but what cold can affect him when Ram protects!

In Kedarnath there is a temple, some shops and residences. A day's stay, and he, on the advice of Ramkinker, travelled onwards. After descending for some miles, the pilgrims commenced to walk up another chain of mountains. Higher and higher again they climbed. Again, glorious enchanting landscapes and scenes met their eyes. At the foot of a hill they came upon a resting place where there was a small tank called Gauri Kund, wherein hot water through a spring is collected. There was also another tank in which the water was yellow in color. From there he and Ramkinker started on their upward journey, miles and miles of ascents were traversed. The pathway now was not so bad as that which led to Kedarnath. For days and days they walked on and at last neared the place called Badrinath or Badrinarayan. While they were yet about half a mile from the place, they sat down on the path and looked at the Badrinath mountains. The sight was bewitching.

To describe the scene the poor pen of Ramdas is quite inadequate and unfit. As he gazed on, he for a time lost body-consciousness and became one with the tall mountains in the midst of which he was sitting. Badrinath is the source of the river Alaknanda. While going up these heights, at three or four places, the pilgrims had to cross wide tracts of snow. He travelled over them with naked feet. These tracts of snow are glaciers. Below the surface of these vast cakes of snow is flowing water in heavy torrents downhill to meet the river below. It is said that many pilgrims, while walking on their surface, have been sucked down by the torrent, some thin layer of snow giving way beneath their feet. The story is current that a wealthy merchant of Bombay, while being carried on a *Doli* or cradle–like conveyance by four strong men, was drowned and lost in the swift current below.

Badrinath was reached—it was a flat valley surrounded on all sides by high mountains like Kedarnath—and here stands the temple of Badrinarayan in white marble. At this place also there was a tank containing hot water, received from a hot spring running down the hills. All the pilgrims bathed in this tank. The cold was very intense. But Ram was kind and gracious at the same time, so Ramdas did not feel the rigor of the cold very much. He had some difficulty in gaining entrance to the temple for the *darshan* of Badrinarayan, as there was a heavy rush of pilgrims at the front door. But some sickly people were permitted to get in by a narrow side door at which two *Pandas* or *Brahmins* were set to watch. He sought entrance here. One of the *Pandas* said:

"If you are sick, you can come in."

"No, Ramdas is not sick," replied Ramdas.

"Well, pretend that you are sick if you are not," suggested the Pandaji.

"Never," returned Ramdas, "he does not want the *darshan* of Badrinath by telling a lie. It is against the command of Ram."

Saying thus, he turned away from the place. But the kind Pandaji at once grasping his hand took him inside and getting him the *darshan* of Badrinath gave him also some *prasad*. O Ram! Thou art testing Thy slave in various ways. Remaining in Badrinath for a day, the sadhus started on their return journey. After several days' walk they came to a place called Ramnagar whence the railway line starts running southward. In all, the distance travelled over the Himalayas was 400 miles, and the time taken from Hardwar to Ramnagar was 40 days.

Ramnagar[1], as the name suggests, is a blessed place. Charity is the ideal of the people there. Near the railway station there was a dispensary, worked by the Congress[2] volunteers for the benefit of ailing pilgrims. Hundreds of pilgrims are every day receiving aid from this dispensary. Arrangements by well-to–do citizens are made for feeding sadhus and poor pilgrims. The people of the place are kind and hos-

---
[1] *Ramnagar*: literally "place of God"
[2] *congress*: political party of the Indian freedom movement

pitable. For his part, Ramdas must say the same with regards to all parts of India wherever he travelled. Ram was uniformly kind to him in all his travels, because he had started on his travels at the bidding of Ram alone.

At Ramnagar, he and Ramkinker got into the train proceeding to Mathura, which they reached in due time. Here Ramkinker, who was taken ill, proposed to return to Jhansi. During all the time he was with Ramdas, Ramkinker was more than a mother to him. He took every care of him. It was all Ram's wish that such a friend should leave him. Accordingly, Ramkinker left Mathura for Jhansi. Ramdas was now alone only for a few minutes, for Ram had another sadhu ready at the *dharmashala* where they were halting, to take him up.

27.

MATHURA, GOKUL AND BRINDABAN

MATHURA IS THE BIRTHPLACE of that great incarnation—Sri Krishna. Sri Krishna is the veritable personification of Love itself. His imperishable name lives still green and in all its pristine glory in the minds of all people in India. *The Bhagavad Gita* stands unrivalled in the depth of its philosophy pointing out the one Goal which all human endeavor should aim at as the ultimate accomplishment of all life and existence. Mathura still remembers vividly the child Krishna and his charmed life, which is proved by the variety of *mandirs* in the place, in which he is worshipped daily in the form of gaudily dressed idols. On the day of Ramdas' arrival at Mathura—Ramkinker being laid up with fever—Ramdas, before he came in touch with the new sadhu–Ram, went to the city in quest of the holy river Jumna. Ram, who was ever ready to offer help to him, now brought him in touch with a *Brahmin* going towards the river. He came of his own accord towards him and proposed to lead him to the river.

Having reached the holy Jumna, Ramdas first washed his clothes and then descended into the river for a bath. But before doing so, he placed his small *lota* on one of the stone steps into which he also put his spectacles. Finishing bath he was returning to the spot where he had placed the *lota*, and he was only a moment too late, because a monkey coming up carried off the spectacles. Now, without spectacles, he could not clearly see objects at a distance. The

Brahmin guide seeing this was annoyed. But Ramdas unperturbed said:

"It was all Ram's wish," and thought within himself that perhaps Ram meant to restore his failing sight.

But the *Brahmin* would not rest content. He requested two boys standing nearby to run after the monkey for the pair of spectacles. The monkey, meanwhile, was jumping from one turret of the temple to the other, closely followed by a number of other monkeys who thought the first one had got some eatable in its grasp. However, in about a quarter of an hour, the boys returned bringing with them the pair of spectacles in a sound condition. It was after all a test of Ram on his humble slave. After visiting some temples of Sri Krishna by the kindness of this *Brahmin* guide, he proceeded next day to Govardhan, in the company of the new sadhu–Ram.

Govardhan was situated at a distance of 14 miles from Mathura. They reached this place at midday. Here was the famous hill of Govardhan which is said to have been lifted by Sri Krishna and supported on the tip of his little finger to protect the cows and cowherds—his playmates—from the heavy torrent of rain sent down by the angry god Indra.[1] But this hill is fast diminishing and has come down almost to the level of the surrounding land. The stones cut out from the hill have been for the most part used in the erection of houses at the place. However to represent the hill, a piece of rock from it is preserved, enclosed by an iron fence and with a top roof. Upon this rock pilgrims pour ghee, milk, curds, etc., and offer *puja*. Even from this rock, bits are knocked off by the pilgrims and carried as mementos. After securing food at a *dharmashala*, Ramdas and the sadhu–Ram rested for a while in the afternoon.

In the evening, both the sadhu–Ram and he were out on the road going about the town when they heard from a distance the sound of *bhajan*. Thither Ram led him and the sadhu–Ram. Shortly after this, they found themselves in a small *Rammandir*,

---

[1] *Indra*: king of the gods in the Hindu pantheon

and in front of the images about half a dozen saints were sitting and singing to the accompaniment of cymbals, tambourine and *mridanga*, the glorious name of Ram. The words were "Hare Ram, Hare Ram, Ram Ram, Hare Hare! Hare Krishna, Hare Krishna, Krishna Krishna, Hare Hare!"

This *bhajan* was sung repeatedly in a variety of tunes, producing in the atmosphere an electric influence full of peace. In this place he remained for nearly four hours fully absorbed in the charming sound of Ram's name. Next day, he and his guide started back for Mathura, and after a short stay there, Ramdas, who missed the sadhu-Ram, proceeded alone to Gokul, lying at a distance of about 5 miles. Ah! Gokul is the place where Sri Krishna grew up as a child, played his games and exhibited his extraordinary powers! Here also the blessed Jumna flows. It was here in the river, perhaps, that Sri Krishna rode and danced on the hood of the venomous serpent Kaliya. After a day's stay here, he returned to Mathura, whence he proceeded to Brindaban about six miles off.

Brindaban is a very delightful place. Here the same Jumna flows in all her tameness and purity. There are beautiful natural gardens of *neem* and other trees on the banks of the river. To sit under their cool shade, when the fresh breeze is blowing over the place from the bosom of mother Jumna, is to enjoy heaven itself. He was charmed with the place and stayed on the banks of the river for a fortnight, made the dry sand his bed and seat for the night, and the shade of the trees a little above, his resting place for the day. Moonlight nights here were all-bewitching. The very air seemed to be charged with the presence of that Love incarnate Sri Krishna—and when soft breezes were blowing they seemed to be carrying into Ramdas' ears the maddening music of Sri Krishna's flute and the silvery sound of the tinkling tiny bells of his blessed dancing feet. Now and again, a deep, soft and resonant voice would travel in the air—"Radheshyam, Radheshyam[2]." Ramdas

---

[2] *Radheshyam*: Radha, an incarnation of the Divine Mother is the consort of Shyam (Krishna). Refers to the mystical union of the manifest and unmanifest aspects of God.

lived there in a state of complete ecstasy and rapture. Days passed by unconsciously. The whole stay seemed to be one long-drawn, sweet and pleasant dream.

At Brindaban, he visited many *Krishna-mandirs* of which the *Ranganath-mandir* is a huge and picturesque structure. It resembles a fortress enclosed by high massive walls. The gateway and interior building and roofs are all made of stone artistically carved. The command came at last from Ram to quit. Returning to Mathura, he got into a train directed by the friends of the place.

28.

RAIPUR

THE TRAIN CARRIED HIM to Raipur. Ram's ways are mysterious. So he did not know why Ram had brought him to Raipur since it is not a place of pilgrimage. After taking his midday meal in the company of a sadhu kindly provided by Ram, at the suggestion of the sadhu–Ram, they went to a beautiful garden of the place. Here after bathing in the water of the canal, Ramdas spread a small deerskin he was carrying with him (presented by a kind friend at Jhansi, of course, supplied by Ram) under the shade of a tree and laying himself down upon it, had hardly closed his eyes, when someone lightly shook him by the shoulders. Opening his eyes he discovered a young Mohammedan beside him.

"Excuse the disturbance, sir," said the young friend in Hindustani[1].

Ramdas now sat up and enquired what he wanted.

"I have come to have a chat with you. I want to know if you have faith in Mohammed," inquired the young friend.

"Why not? He is one of the greatest prophets of God," replied Ramdas.

"Why do you say, one of the prophets?—why not the *only* one?" put in the Muslim friend.

"Young brother, although Mohammed is a world Teacher, there are others also who are as great Teachers, for instance,

---
[1] *Hindustani*: the Indian language, Hindi, widely spoken in the North

Buddha, Jesus Christ and Krishna—and in our days—Mahatma Gandhi. If you would try to understand the message they deliver to the world, you will find that in the essentials they all agree and hold out the same goal to mankind."

The words produced a deep impression upon the mind of the Muslim friend. The conversation continued for some time with regard to Ramdas' experiences, etc. The young friend became very fond of him, so much so, that he made up his mind to follow Ramdas wherever he went. It was a sudden impulse. Ramdas told him that he should not do so as he had no orders from Ram to take him with him. After some persuasion he was induced to give up the idea. But he wanted something from Ramdas as a memento. Ramdas told him that he was quite willing to give him anything he had with him—that he had only to ask for what he wanted. The kind friend then asked for the deerskin and it was at once handed over to him. He said, while receiving it:

"My object in having this skin is to perform my *namaz*—i.e., prayers to Allah, sitting upon it; and it will also remind me of you every time."

At parting he asked Ramdas where he was going next. He replied that Ram intended to take him to Ajmere.

"Well, that is good," said the friend. "When you are there, please don't fail to pay a visit to the famous Muslim shrine, the Khaja Pir. Any Mussulman can show you the way to it."

These were prophetic words. In due course he reached Ajmere. It was night. While he was resting in the station along with some other sadhus, who had also arrived by the same train, the railway police objected and asked all of them to go out. He sought a place under a tree in front of the station within the compound. But here again the policeman interfered and drove him away. Knocking about for some time, he saw at last a spot under another tree in a far-off corner of the railway compound. As he had nothing to spread on the floor, he lay himself down on the bare ground. When his nose came in close proximity with the ground he felt the strong smell of urine. O Ram, how kind you are; you make your humble slave pass through every kind of experience—all for his good.

This condition taught him further still what a folly it was to make much of this perishable body, and it also tended greatly to make him find his true level, which is indeed very, very low. To afford him the benefit of this experience, O Ram, Thou alone appeared as the policeman and brought about this circumstance. Here Ramdas, the child of Ram, slept soundly till morning in the loving embrace of that all-powerful Being—Ram.

29.

Ajmere

AT DAYBREAK, he directed his steps towards the city. When he was going through the thickly populated streets of Ajmere, knowing not where he was being led—he was always engaged in the contemplation of Ram—a tall and stout Mohammedan stopped Ramdas and made a sign to follow him. He had no choice in such matters. He always thinks that all calls are from Ram. So, without any hesitation he obeyed the Mohammedan guide, not knowing nor caring to know where the friend was taking him. They walked through the streets for nearly a mile and at last stopped at an arched gate. The friend entered closely followed by him. After passing through a courtyard, and on descending some flight of steps, and then going through a doorway, a beautiful *masjid*[1] came into view. Going in here, he found himself in front of a huge silver *mandap*[2] or *tabooth*, domed and carved picturesquely.

"This is Khaja Pir," exclaimed the Muslim friend. "Kneel down here and enlist yourself as the *chela*[3] of Mohammed."

At once Ramdas knelt as bidden by him, in all reverence. Then looking up to the kind friend, he said:

"Brother, there is no need of his enlisting himself here as Mohammed's *chela*, because he has already been a *chela* of Mohammed."

---
[1] *masjid*: mosque
[2] *mandap*: altar, enclosure for shrine
[3] *chela*: disciple

O Ram—O Mohammed! how wonderful are Thy ways! In fulfillment of the fervent wish of that young Muslim friend of Raipur, Thou hadst brought Ramdas on a visit to the sacred shrine of the Mohammedans. All glory to Thee, O Ram—O Mohammed!

Leading him out of this holy place, the Muslim friend left him on the main road. Soon after this, he was taken up by a *sannyasi* named Swami Ramachandra—a man of pure and tender heart. He became greatly attached to Ramdas and undertook to look after him in every way. O Ram! How can Thy ignorant slave understand Thy ways! He knows only this much—Thou art all kindness, all love. First the Swamiji inquired in the bazaar for an *annakshetra*, and having received the information and got two meal-chits, took him there; and after finishing meals, led him to a rest house where he shared his meager bedding with Ramdas in spite of his remonstrances. His kindness to the poor slave of Ram was indeed unbounded.

O Ram—it is Thyself who appearest in the form of these guides to lead, feed and take care of Thy slave. Why, for that matter, Ramdas has now come to look upon all human beings, all creatures, all life, all things as nothing but the manifestation of the Divine Ram, whom he is meditating upon day and night. The Swamiji and he remained in Ajmere for three days, and then left for Pushkar Raj. Travelling on the hill for about five miles, they reached a large natural reservoir of water, on one side of which were erected temples and *dharmashalas*. The Swamiji and he occupied one of them. Here Ramdas spent five days in *bhajan* of Sri Ram. Swami Ramachandra had to stay in Pushkar Raj for some days more.

So Ramdas, at Ram's command, left the place alone for Ajmere, where he secured the company of a sadhu. Prevented from travelling by train by Ram's will, they walked for about 16 miles and then got into a train. The sadhu-Ram who was complaining of indigestion at Ajmere recovered his health completely by this walk of 16 miles, receiving on the way very little food. Ram does everything for the best. At a junction named Mehsana the sadhus met another *sannyasi* at whose suggestion they accompanied him to a station called Dharmapuri, where, alighting, they walked straight to the *ashram* of a sadhu residing near the *mandir* of Mahadev. The sadhu gave a hearty welcome to the guests and provided them with accommodation, food, etc.

Ramdas was pressed to remain in that *ashram* for some days. But, as the sadhu–Ram could not do so, he left the place after a stay of two days and proceeded on his journey. A week passed in this *ashram* when two *sannyasis* from a neighboring village came there on a visit, and took him to their *ashram* which was in a jungle. He remained in this jungle which he found best suited for *Ram-bhajan*. The *sannyasis* were very kind to him. In this jungle there was a small *mandir* of Narahari[4]. The interior of this *mandir* was a perfect square—the sides corresponding exactly to Ramdas' height. Except for one or two hours of sleep in the night, he was repeating the whole night the glorious *mantram* of Sri Ram. Here, he proved for himself beyond all doubt that Ram protects with the greatest of care the devotees who entirely trust Him and solely depend upon Him.

The jungle was infested with wild pigs, serpents, scorpions and other venomous creatures. Every night a herd of about 20 to 30 wild pigs would surround the *mandir*, the door of which was always open. The wild animals would come to dig out roots with their snouts from the marshy land surrounding the *mandir*, for these roots were their food. Ramdas was freely going out in the nights when they were about. But by Ram's grace they never harmed him. The villagers who were coming there during the day would warn him of the ferocious nature of these wild beasts. But complete trust in Ram means full protection and no fear. Moreover day and night the *mandir* was freely visited by long black serpents, none of which, how-

---

[4] *Narahari*: an incarnation of Lord Vishnu

ever, molested him. Again every morning when he lifted up the gunny or sack piece spread for him by the kind *sannyasis* as *asan* or seat—which Ramdas would use also for a bed at night—he would discover beneath it a number of reddish yellow scorpions. But none of these stung him.

O Ram! When Thy loving arm is ever ready to protect Thy humble slave, who could harm him? Thou art, O Ram, everywhere—in all creatures—the whole universe and all in it is Thy own manifestation. O Ram—all glory to Thee! Ramdas, by Ram's command, remained in this jungle for about a month and a half. The afternoons were mostly spent in the society of cowherd boys who would come to this forest for grazing cattle. They would play upon flutes and give him the pleasure of listening to their sweet music. These boys appeared to him as so many cheerful, active, little Krishnas. By Ram's grace the stay there proved altogether a most delightful one.

On one occasion, the kind *sannyasi* friend took him on a visit to a village, several stations away from Dharmapuri—the name of which is Yadavpur. Here there was a great congregation of sadhus. There were in all about 200 in number. It was a feast of *satsang*[5]; the beauty of it all was to observe the unstinted hospitality of the villagers. Every article of comfort which they possessed was at the disposal of the sadhus. One day Ram's command came to Ramdas to move on. Accordingly he left the jungle against the wishes of the *sannyasis*, who wanted him to remain for some months more. Ram passed him on to the care of a merchant at the railway station, who undertook to escort him as far as the merchant travelled. An incident that took place here requires to be related now.

---

[5] *satsang*: association of people devoted to God or a saint

30.

MONEY IS THE ROOT OF ALL EVIL

WHEN THE MERCHANT and Ramdas were entering the train, there was a heavy rush of passengers and so the merchant had to push his way in the thick of the crowd in order to get into a carriage, which he did, followed by Ramdas. He had scarcely settled himself down on a seat when the merchant friend came to him and informed:

"Maharaj, somebody has robbed me of my leather purse containing fifteen rupees and the railway ticket."

And he showed his waistcoat pocket, the inside lining of which was found to have been neatly cut out for the removal of the purse. It must all have been the work of a few seconds. The merchant continued to say:

"Now what shall I do? I have neither ticket nor money. May I report the matter to the railway police?" The train was about to start.

"Since you ask for his advice," said Ramdas, "he requests you to keep mum over the affair. No good fretting or making a fuss over the matter. As regards the ticket, you may travel to your destination without one. On the way or at the alighting station, if the ticket is demanded of you by the railway officers, you can explain to them the way you lost the purse and the ticket. As a proof of this, you may show them the torn vest pocket."

This advice of humble Ramdas did not satisfy the merchant. He could not rest content until he reported the matter to the railway police. Now a police officer came to the compartment and commenced teasing many poorly dressed and unassuming sadhus, compelling them to hand over their bags and bundles for inspection. Not finding anything with them, the policeman's attention was next directed towards a group of simple dressed villagers whose big turbans were all pulled down and their coats and clothing rummaged. On the person of one of them was at length discovered a sum of Rupees 20. This man was now asked by the police a number of sharp and suspicious questions as to how he came in possession of the money. He explained that he was only a keeper of the amount belonging to all the friends of that group. By this time, the merchant-friend who was looking upon the inquiry set on foot by him, had got disgusted with it all and was in a penitent mood, because he saw that many innocent people were being harassed for the sake of his loss. The money found upon the villagers and their tickets also were wrested from them and kept by the police, and were only returned to the owners after they had passed several stations. Meanwhile, the incident caused a great deal of annoyance and anxiety. Now the merchant came to Ramdas, and giving him a *namaskar*[1], said:

"Maharaj, fool that I was not to have listened to your golden advice. Behold, what a mess I have made of the whole matter. To how many innocent men I have caused pain. Pardon thy slave."

"Pray, sue pardon of Ram, O friend," was Ramdas' only reply. By this occurrence Ram taught Ramdas a beautiful moral—that he should not commit at any time the blunder of carrying or owning money which means nothing but trouble and mischief. Rightly it is said: "Money is the root of all evil."

---

[1] *namaskar*: a salutation, literally "I honor God within you"

31.

JUNAGAD

NOW THE TRAIN carried Ramdas to the Junagad station. It was midday. He was without a guide. At the city gate he inquired of a policeman if there was a *Ram-mandir* in that place. He replied that there was a *Ram-mandir* about two miles from the gate and he pointed out the way leading to it. Ramdas walked on, making frequent inquiries on the way. At last, he reached the high gateway of the *Ram-mandir*. Entering, he was welcomed by the *mahant*[1] of the *ashram*, with whom he remained for about a week. Here he had the benefit of the society of six other sadhus who were also there as the guests of the kind-hearted *mahant*. All of them were very kind to Ramdas.

Ram here performed two wonderful miracles—one of these sadhus had an attack of fever from a fortnight, and in spite of various kinds of treatment he was as bad as ever. He was bedridden, emaciated and pale. Besides, he was disheartened and was fretting over his illness. Seeing his condition, Ramdas could not resist going to his bed, and sitting near him and offering himself for his service, began pressing his legs lightly. Coming to know of this the ailing sadhu sat up and remonstrated, saying that he was quite unworthy to receive such attention from him. He only asked for a blessing from Ramdas that he should be all right by the following day. Ram-

---
[1] *mahant*: abbot of ashram

das said that he was only a humble slave of Ram and had no right to bless anybody.

"Do bless in the name of Ram," he appealed.

"Well, brother," said Ramdas, "may Sri Ram, the Protector of all, bless you with health by tomorrow morning."

That night Ram was perhaps busy setting the sadhu right, for next morning he was entirely free from fever and was moving about in good cheer and health. This marvelous cure by Ram, for working which he had made humble Ramdas his tool, made quite a sensation in the *ashram*. So he became the object of considerable attention and love from all in the *ashram*. About three or four days later, another sadhu fell ill. He too asked Ramdas to bless him in the same way as he had done the other one. Ramdas prayed again to Ram as requested. O Ram, what a powerful being Thou art! The second sadhu also recovered by the following morning. All glory to Thee, Ram!

Ramdas was not made to remain in this *ashram* long. He met one day the same *sannyasi* who had guided him to Dharmapuri. He had evinced a great liking for Ramdas. Now he took him up and brought him to another *ashram*, belonging to a well-known *sannyasi* of Junagad, Kashigirji by name. In this *ashram* or *akhada*, as it was called, Ramdas was loved by all *sannyasis*—there were about fifteen of them. Ram's intention in taking him to Junagad was to enable him to scale the heights of the famous hill of Girnar—the seat of Guru Dattatreya and Mother Ambaji. He expressed this wish to Kashigirji who proposed also to accompany him on his climb. Ram's kindness is indeed very great. A day was fixed and one night he mounted the steps of Girnar with Kashigirji and six other *sannyasis* who were also in the party. The total number of steps to be mounted in order to reach the summit of the hills was about 9000. Six thousand steps were covered, and they reached, at about three after midnight, the *ashram* of a *sannyasi* whose name was Shankargirji.

Here a halt was made for the night. Cold on the hill was severe. Ram was kind and his *bhajan* was so sweet. Next morning, the party climbed further up and reached first the temple of Mother Ambaji and thence ascending a flight of steps mounted again the highest peak among those hills. While nearing this peak, the steps were irregular and slippery, but Ram led all up safely. Here on the summit are the footprints of Guru Dattatreya. Hundreds of pilgrims are every day ascending these hills for the *darshan* of these holy footprints. To sit on the edge of this peak and to have a sweeping look all around is to present to the gaze a most enthralling sight. The charming landscapes on all sides—the distant hills painted with green and yellow—the vast blue expanse of the sky overhead, and the thin silvery streaks of sparkling water streaming down the smooth and shining sides of rocks—are all scenes that elevate the looker-on to regions at once mystic and celestial.

On getting down this hill—halfway—the party visited some caves occupied by *mahatmas* and had the uncommon pleasure of their society. Then were visited the various reservoirs of water on the slopes of the hills. At length they returned at noon to the hospitable *ashram* of Shankargirji. After dinner the party started on their downward journey and reached Junagad in the evening. Next day all the *sannyasis* of the party were complaining of stiffness and pain in their limbs. Some of them, for two or three days, could only hobble along. But Ram was so kind to Ramdas that he did not feel any pain or stiffness in his legs. Now Ram made him acquainted with two young friends Maganlal and Kantilal, both of whom conceived a great love for him. In their company he spent a few very happy days. They would take him every evening for walks in the public gardens and among groves of trees.

Once in their company Ramdas ascended a small hill called Lakshman Tekri. They also introduced him to some Muslim friends of the place who were all very kind to him. A visit was paid to the Datar Mosque at the foot of the Datar hills. Maganlal made him acquainted with several friends of Junagad who were all uniformly kind to Ramdas. Maganlal arranged for his journey to Somanath, a noted shrine of great historical importance. Ramdas duly proceeded to this shrine in the company of a Gujarati[2] friend who met him at the railway station by the grace of Ram.

This friend on reaching Veraval station, as arranged by Maganlal, took him to the house of a rich merchant of the place—a relation of Maganlal. But when Ramdas visited him, he was laid up with high fever and his whole household was in a state of acute anxiety over his illness. He sat near the sick friend and touching him on the arm felt the high temperature. Before leaving the room, Ramdas was asked by his relatives present, as well as by the friends who escorted him to the place, to bless the patient with health. Accordingly Ramdas said that by the grace of almighty Ram he would be all right next morning.

Ram manifested His power here as well! The patient was entirely free from all fever next morning. He was having the attack of fever for five days past without intermission. By Ram's grace, now the fever having left him, he was able to walk out to his place of business. Ramdas was staying in the topmost story of his shop—a huge building. Here too all were kind to him. He duly visited the ruins and the temple of Somanath. The underground cave, in which there is the huge image of Somanath, was entered and he stood before the idol. Here again he felt thrills of ecstasy in the presence of Somanath. He bathed in the river a little away from the temple. Returning to Veraval, Ramdas expressed to the merchant-friend, as prompted by Ram, his wish to visit Prachi and Muddi Goraknath, and said that he would go on foot early next morning.

"No, Swamiji," said the kind merchant, "you should not go on foot. I shall engage a bullock cart for you, for the road leading to these places is so rugged and rough that even a horse carriage cannot be driven over there. Moreover, you have to cover a distance of 16 miles, which is a long distance for a weak man like you to walk through."

---

[2] *Gujarati*: a person from the Indian state of Gujarat

Although Ramdas was against the proposal, he was prevailed upon by the friend to sit in a cart along with some other friends who were also bound for Prachi. The kind friend dropped into his pocket a small kerchief to which were tied Rupees 2 for cart-hire to and from Prachi. The cart started before daybreak. They had not travelled half a mile, when Ramdas saw the driver beating the bullocks with a heavy stick. He, of course, could not bear the sight. He felt as if the blows were delivered on his own back. He appealed to the driver not to inflict injury on the bullock. He replied that the bullocks would not go if they were not chastised. Ram now commanded Ramdas to give up the cart at once. After paying Re. 1, his hire, he got down and walked the distance and reached Prachi about midday.

As he was proceeding, he happened to pass close to a poorly dressed man with a bundle on his back. Seeing Ramdas he quickly moved out of the way and began walking at the other end of the road. Proceeding a little further, he met another man coming from the opposite direction, and both greeted each other with 'Ram, Ram.' After going a little further Ramdas questioned him why he was moving so far away from him, to which he replied that he was a pariah.

"O, but you are Ramdas' brother, all the same." So saying, Ramdas approached him and took him by the hand. He stared at Ramdas in confusion.

"I am a *dhed*[3] by caste," he again said.

"Ramdas is your brother," repeated Ramdas. "A man who has the name of Ram on his lips is superior to a *Brahmin*—in the eyes of Ram, all are equal."

Until he parted, Ramdas went on talking to him about the glory of Ram. Now he took a sidetrack and separated from Ramdas, who then fell into the company of a Mohammedan friend driving a horse loaded with some merchandise. This friend, whose nature was simple and childlike, gave him much

---
[3] *dhed*: kind of untouchable

pleasure by his society until Ramdas reached Prachi. Bathing in the large tank into which a river was flowing, he visited several *mandirs*, met two sadhus of the place, and then started on his return journey, and reached in the evening the shrine called Muddi Goraknath. Here he remained for a night in the society of the sadhus of the temple, which is also a cave, entrance to which can only be gained by descending a number of stone steps.

Starting from there early next morning he reached Veraval in the forenoon. The first thing he did was to return the balance of Re. 1 to the merchant. He had walked all the way with enthusiasm, repeating according to his wont, the sacred *Ram–mantram*. The following day he went back by train to Junagad. Maganlal and Kantilal heartily welcomed him back. They pressed him to remain in Junagad for some days more. He agreed to do so, by Ram's will, provided he was allowed to remain in solitude where he could spend his days in entire devotion to and meditation of Ram. Accordingly Ram Himself pitched upon a place called Muchkund Rishi's *ashram*. This is situated right in the midst of a dense jungle over a hill, on the way to Girnar, about 4 miles from Junagad. There is a temple here in ruins, besides a number of *samadhis* in a neglected condition. The place has consequently a weird appearance.

32.

MUCHKUND RISHI'S ASHRAM AND DWARKA

RAMDAS OCCUPIED this *ashram* and remained in it for 10 days. He would light a small fire and squatting before it perform *Ram-bhajan* all the night. The place was full of bats and doves. Since it was a deserted and frightful place, the people of the town and sadhus were considering it a privilege to visit the *sannyasi* dwelling in such a place. Some of these well-intentioned friends at first apprised him of the supposed fears of the place. They were all told that when the all-powerful Ram protects, there was no room for any fear. Here Maganlal and Kantilal were paying him visits daily. They procured for him from Muslim friends an excellent translation of the Holy Quran in English by a well-known Moulvi of Lahore. The Quran is indeed a grand work. Ramdas derived great benefit by a study of these teachings of the great Prophet Mohammed.

Then Ramdas received the command from Ram to leave the place. Accordingly he left Junagad by the midnight train and, after a change at some junction, reached the station of Porbundar. From the station he went to the city of Sudamapuri. The blessed saint Sudama, the great *bhakta* of Sri Krishna, had lived here and hence the name Sudamapuri. Here he was reminded now and again of Sudama's humble offer of beaten rice to Krishna and the loving acceptance of it by Him, and also how Sri Krishna on one occasion washed the feet of Sudama, which brought to Ramdas' mind the famous line of Swami Rama Tirtha: "A slave is a slave because he is free."

In the company of two sadhus, he visited the temple of Sri Krishna, said to have been erected at the spot where Sudama's cottage once stood. The same evening he and the two sadhus, who were joined later by two more, in all forming a party of five, started on foot towards Dwarka. It was quite a jolly party of whom an old, bearded sadhu—with a big turban on his head, a thick *kambal*[1] on his back, a pair of wooden sandals in one hand and a broken brass pot in the other, a wooden arm-rester hanging by the shoulder, a quilt jacket on his body, and a *kaupin* around his loins—was chosen the leader of the company. He was a simple, unassuming, good-natured and harmless old saint. Merrily the sadhus walked mile after mile, each narrating to the other some bits of experiences. Ramdas was all the time engaged either in listening to the stories or repeating Rams' sweet name. A halt was made for the night in a small wayside village, the residents of which treated the sadhus with great hospitality.

Next morning, very early, the sadhu-Ram, the leader, gave the call for a start. Shaking off sleep, the sadhus rose and, shouldering their respective bundles, set forth on their journey. Thus they travelled on, breaking journey at midday and at night in villages, until they reached the old shrine called Muladwarka, covering in all a distance of 20 miles from Sudamapuri. Here, there was an *ashram* of a sadhu in which was found always an assembly of twenty to thirty itinerant sadhus. Here the new arrivals mingled with the sadhus of the *ashram* in happy association, and then visited the old temple. It is said Sri Krishna had made his first stay at this place before he changed to Dwarka proper, or Bet Dwarka, as it is called.

After travelling a little further the party reached Gomati Dwarka. This shrine is also considered an important place of pilgrimage on account of the sacred river Gomati which flowed here at one time but has since dried up. Now remains,

---

[1] *kambal*: blanket

in place of it, a tank in which pilgrims consider it a great merit to bathe. After obtaining *darshan* in the big temple of this place and spending a day there in the society of many other travelling sadhus, who visit in hundreds every day, the party strode on under the orders and lead of the venerable sadhu–Ram. Arriving at the railway station, they got into a train which was already fully occupied by other sadhus. This carriage was called "Sitaram" carriage. It was really generous of the railway company to permit sadhus to travel on this line free of charge. It was an uncommon blessing of Ram to have secured for Ramdas the company of nearly forty sadhus, all mixing with each other in perfect amity and innocence like small children at play. Each sadhu was busy opening his bundle or bag to exhibit to his neighbor sadhu his articles or curios, such as conches, shells, *rudraksha*[2], small framed pictures of gods of various shrines, all collected during his pilgrimage all over India.

At last the train carried them to the railway terminus—a small station. Alighting here, they proceeded to the seashore where they were allowed to board two steamboats belonging to a Mohammedan. When the permission was granted by the boat-owner, there was a cry from all sadhus in one voice— "Mohammed Ki Jai!" The gulf was duly crossed and the sadhus reached the island of Dwarka. It was night when they arrived. Resting in a *dharmashala* for the night, the next morning the party visited the famous temple of Dwarkanath. An indescribable feeling of rapture and joy was experienced by Ramdas when he stood in front of the idol of Sri Krishna. He remained inside the temple for nearly two hours in a state of complete and blissful abstraction. He next wandered on the seashore, jumping from rock to rock, all the time absorbed in the meditation of Ram. The party of sadhus stayed here for two days. On the third day, at the command of the sadhu–Ram, the company started on their return journey.

---

[2] *rudraksha*: a sacred seed, used in rosaries

Now an incident occurred which must be noted down. The party as usual stopped at a certain village for the night and at the command of the leader all started before daybreak. The sadhu-Ram awoke rather too early. It was still dark—and the sadhus grumbled that they could not properly see their way. There were also two more sadhus who had joined the party at the village. These were young men—one of them totally blind led by the other who was blind in one eye. The sadhu-Ram assured the party that the sun would rise soon. But for nearly two hours they walked on in the dark, stumbling, grumbling and missing the way now and again—still daybreak was as far off as ever. They all took the leader severely to task, but the old sadhu-Ram was silently treading the path and did not vouchsafe any reply to the adverse criticism passed by his friends. He was himself groping in the dark with great difficulty and was at every step becoming more and more conscious of the fact that he had lost the way, and that he was leading all in an unknown direction.

On and on the party went. Now they came upon wet ground, then on muddy soil. Farther and farther they went and at last found themselves in mud knee-deep. Now there was a furious cry of halt from all. It was yet pitch dark. Everyone was straining his eyes—except of course the poor blind sadhu—towards the horizon in expectation of signs of the rising sun. But the sun was still a long way off. Again some of the sadhus grumbled and asked the sadhu-Ram as to what they should do next. The sadhu-Ram never replied. After fruitless discussion for some time, they arrived at the unanimous conclusion that they should wait there until daybreak, for to attempt to move might invite a worse fate—perhaps a fall into a ditch or a deeper descent into mud.

33.

BOMBAY

So ABOUT AN HOUR was spent standing in that morass in severe cold. At length, the flaming chariot of the Sun-god came speeding up the horizon, heralding a day of hope and joy. Most of the sadhus of the party were now determined to abandon the leadership of the sadhu-Ram, and forming groups of two amongst themselves moved away from the place. But Ramdas, who was all through as silent as a top—busy with the repetition of Ram's name—clung fast to the sadhu-Ram, helped him in carrying his sandals and *lota* and followed him. Although for a time the sadhus were separated, they all met again at the nearest railway station. Here all of them got into the train going northward. At Viramgam a change had to be made. In the rush of passengers, Ramdas and the sadhu-Ram missed each other and did not meet again. Probably the sadhu-Ram, who wanted to proceed to Mathura, must have boarded a train travelling still northward. Ramdas with some other sadhus got into a train going towards Bombay. Ram's kindness was so great that the train he sat in happened to be one that travelled directly to Bombay without requiring any change on the way.

The train had almost neared Ahmedabad when, at a certain station, a ticket inspector came in to check tickets. He found about half a dozen sadhus in the carriage without tickets, of whom Ramdas was, of course, one. He gave an order that all sadhus should get down. Accordingly, one by one, the sadhus dropped down from the carriage. Now Ramdas also rose up, but the ticket inspector who was standing quite close to him, placing his hand on the shoulder of Ramdas, pressed him to sit again saying:

"Maharaj, you need not alight. What I said was not meant for you."

O Ram, why this preference for Ramdas? No, he has no right to question Thee. Thy slave is ever bound to Thy holy feet—O Ram—and that is all. After passing Ahmedabad, some friends in the carriage provided him with fruits, etc. He found later that all passengers about him in the carriage were very kind to him, although he was all along silent, but only repeating Ram's name under breath. About 8 o'clock in the evening, the train reached the Grant Road station in Bombay. Here, coming out of the station, Ramdas, as prompted by Ram, proceeded directly to Bhuleshwar. For the way he had to make enquiries now and again as he walked on. Now arriving at the temple, he rested for the night on one of the stone steps of the inner temple. Here, close to the temple, there was a big storied *dharmashala*, instituted in the name of a generous mother—Janakibai.

The *dharmashala* was always full. It could accommodate two to three hundred sadhus. About 4 o'clock in the morning Ramdas, who was asleep, woke up to listen to a most rapturous song issuing from the *dharmashala*. The subject of the song was Radha-Krishna. The manner in which the two devout mothers were singing was full of pathos, and the voices filled the air with a sweet fascinating charm. Krishna's own love seemed to have mingled with the music of their voices. Ramdas felt himself raised to heights of ecstasy and was lost in it as long as the singing lasted.

The day broke. Finishing his bath at the water-tap, Ramdas had just returned to his seat when he was presented by a friend with a chit or ticket and was asked to accompany six other sadhus who held similar chits.

"You are all invited by a merchant for dinner at his residence," he said.

So all the seven sadhus followed this guide who led them through several streets until they were brought to the entrance of the host's house. Since there was still time for dinner, the sadhus sat down under the shade of the trees in the compound. Ramdas had just sat down on a log of wood when a sadhu approaching him said:

"Swamiji, the ticket which was given to me is lost on the way. I have been going without food for two days. Shall I be able to secure dinner without a ticket?"

The only response which Ram made Ramdas to give at the time was to silently and cheerfully hand over to him his own chit and instantly walk out of the place. He now wandered in the sun like a mad man—why say *like* a mad man? He was really mad—mad of Ram. He walked and walked. Unconsciously he directed his steps to the Fort and wandered from one street to another. At a certain turning on the footpath, a grief-stricken man of middle age saluted Ramdas and offered him a *pice*. Returning the salute, he said that he would not accept money but would take fruits. At hand there was a mother selling plantains. The friend bought one plantain for the *pice* and handed it to Ramdas.

Now he made Ramdas sit on the path, and narrated his story. He said that he had only one son who was a veritable jewel. He was so intelligent, so mild, so good in character, so promising, so affectionate and loving and also so handsome in features—such a model of perfection—and this son was carried away by plague about a month ago. Ever since this heavy loss, he had been stricken mad over the sad blow. He therefore begged Ramdas to find a way for him to bear this calamity. Ramdas then replied:

"Brother, to sorrow over the loss of your son is to hug delusion. To be free from this sorrow means to know the reality. There is only one way to wake up to this Reality and that is to meditate upon God."

"How can I do it? I cannot control the mind," put in the friend.

"Well now, begin here to repeat the *mantram* which Ramdas is bidden by Ram to give you and see the immediate effect."

Saying thus, he gave him the *upadesh* of *Ram-mantram* and made him repeat it then and there for about 15 minutes without stopping. While he was doing this, a sense of relief came to him. Then he rose and saluting Ramdas said that he had secured the right key to unlock the gates of peace. He further admitted that since repeating the *mantram* he had been experiencing calmness and he would not give up repeating it always. Then he left the place. Ramdas continued his mad walk.

Now he passed through the broad road adjoining the Port Trust buildings and docks. He went on and on—now going into a maze of streets and lanes—then passing over bridges and railway crossings. At last he found himself about 3 p.m. in front of a building which was familiar to him. Looking up, he discovered the sign board of brother[1] Ramakrishna Rao—portrait painter by profession. Ram prompted him to get up the staircase and in a few minutes he was in the front room occupied by the artist-brother. He was welcomed by the brother most heartily. With this brother he remained for four days. The members of his household were also very kind to him.

During his stay here, Ramdas was utilizing the morning for visiting the various temples of Bombay and the sadhus residing near the temples. He spent one night on the footsteps of the large tank of the Wakeshwar temple, keeping awake almost the whole night in *Ram-bhajan*. By Ram's command, then, he proposed to start.

The kind brother Ramakrishna Rao escorted him as far as the railway station, and, getting him a ticket for Nasik, saw him sit in the night train. Ramakrishna Rao's anxiety for his comforts was so great that he pressed him to take a small packet containing plantains, oranges and some sweets. The train started. Ram now got Ramdas the company of another friend who was sitting beside him on the same bench. He trav-

---

[1]*brother*: Ramdas' actual brother

elled with Ramdas as far as two stations this side of Nasik. All the way he was talking of nothing else but Ram. Now and again he would sing about Ram—composing songs extempore. In fact, he was more mad of Ram than Ramdas himself. Here Ram was teaching Ramdas how to become really mad of him. It was a perfect delight to enjoy his talk and songs of Ram. It was all Ram's preordained plan and Ram is always kind. Before alighting, this friend requested another passenger (who was close to him and who too was bound for Nasik) to guide and take care of Ramdas.

In due time Nasik was reached. The new friend guided him out of the station. Here finding a motor-tram waiting, the friend got into it beckoning to him, and Ramdas followed suit. Soon the tram was full of passengers and the bell sounding, it started. The tram conductor, after clipping tickets for other passengers, came to Ramdas and demanded fee for the ticket. Ramdas had, of course, no money and so nothing to say in reply; while a number of passengers sitting near him in almost one voice told the conductor not to bother the sadhu, as he was not supposed to possess money, and that he should be allowed to sit in the car. Of course, the conductor yielded to their appeal on behalf of Ramdas.

About 3 miles were passed when a ticket inspector got in. He was an elderly man with whiskers. Coming to Ramdas he asked for ticket, but Ramdas having no ticket, the inspector began to fret and worry over it saying that the sadhu could not be allowed to travel free. When he was thus complaining, the same friends who had pleaded for Ramdas with the conductor again spoke for him, but could produce no impression on the inspector. So the only course open for Ramdas was to get down. Accordingly, standing up, he requested the inspector to stop the car so that he might alight. Here again, Ram's power prevailed. The attitude of the inspector now suddenly changed. He told him not to trouble himself and that he might continue the journey in the tram. Ram's tests are at all times coming unawares. One should always be prepared for them and face all vicissitudes calmly and in complete resignation to His will. Then there is no sorrow, no disappointment, no fear of any kind.

34.

PANCHAVATI AND TAPOVAN

PANCHAVATI WAS REACHED. Ramdas saw the beautiful river Godavari, on the banks of which there are a number of *kshetras* for feeding sadhus, *Brahmins* and poor pilgrims. To one of these he directed his steps. On the veranda of a *kshetra* he found a number of *bairagis*[1], mendicant mothers and children. Here he, as prompted by Ram, opened the parcel of fruits, etc., given to him by brother Ramakrishna Rao, and emptied the cloth in which they were tied by distributing them all amongst the small children in that place. This relieved him of a pretty heavy burden. Ram's order is always not to worry about food and clothing. Then Ramdas, going up to the holy river, washed his clothes and after bath sat down on the bank for meditation of Ram. Time passed and it was past midday when he rose and proceeded towards a *dharmashala* and found, on entering, a number of sadhus and others coming out of the front door to wash their hands after dinner. Ramdas quietly sat outside all the time, busy with the repetition of Ram's name. Now a rough-looking man approached him and sitting beside him, asked Ramdas if he had his meal, to which he, of course, replied in the negative.

"Well, come on," he said, "I shall take you to a place where you can get a meal."

---

[1] *bairagis*: kind of monks who live very austerely

And then taking Ramdas by the hand, he conducted him a short distance away on the same road, and entered a high building where he made enquiries if it was possible to give food to a sadhu. The friend who was asked this question on the veranda of the house went in to ascertain the matter. Meanwhile, the guide who took Ramdas there said:

"Look here, Maharaj, you need have no anxiety about food. I shall see that you get a meal without fail even if it is not available here."

"When *Ram-bhajan* is on the lips of Ramdas, he is always far from such anxieties," replied Ramdas.

Later, meals were offered at this *kshetra*. Ram takes care at every step. His concern for his devotees is a thousand times more keen and lively than that of the mother for her new-born baby. Ram now handed Ramdas into the hands of a retired merchant staying in the *dharmashala*, who became very much attached to him. At midnight, without his knowledge, this kind friend would cover Ramdas with a blanket, since he would not accept a *kambal* when offered. The cold on the banks of the Godavari at this time was extreme. At the pressure of this merchant-friend, Ramdas remained with him for two days. During the second night, the friend questioned him if he had cultivated powers of inducing dreams. Ramdas replied that he was quite ignorant of that *sadhana* and he only knew how to utter the name of Ram.

"You can do it if you only wish, Guruji," said the friend. "Just, for instance, desire intensely to know from Ram the winning numbers of the next Derby Sweep, and the number will be made known to you in a dream."

"Ramdas requires none and nothing else but Ram," replied Ramdas.

"You see, the amount that might be won is not for selfish purposes, but for feeding sadhus," suggested the friend.

"Ram sees to the feeding of the sadhus" returned Ramdas.

The friend then became silent. This was again a test of Ram to find out if Ramdas could be tempted to wish for wealth.

Another incident was this. In the *dharmashala* there was a sick girl ailing from fever for about four months. Ramdas was asked by the mother of the girl to pray to Ram for her welfare. Accordingly, going up to her bed and finding her in high fever, he appealed to Ram to bless her with health. Ram's ways are always inscrutable. The girl-mother seemed to have improved for about two days, but again fell ill. Ram alone knows the why and the wherefore.

Next day at noon, Ramdas walked about 3 miles and reached a place called Tapovan. This is said to have been the spot where Lakshmana, brother of Sri Ramachandra, cut the nose of the she-monster Surpanakha. Tapovan is a charming place. Here the clear water of Godavari is flowing at the foot of low hills. To sit on one of these hills is to view a most attractive scene all around. Here, on a large rock, are cut out a number of rectangular caves side by side. About 10 feet from the bottom of the rock at which the water of the river is rushing along, Ramdas fixed upon a cave for a night's *bhajan* and accordingly, after bathing in the river, climbed up and occupied it. The night was intensely cold, so he had not had a wink of sleep. He sat up the whole night repeating the sacred name of Ram. In Tapovan he had occasion to meet several sadhus. Next morning he returned to Panchavati and remained here for a day.

35.

Trimbakeshwar

Early the following morning, Ramdas started for Trimbakeshwar, 16 miles from Panchavati. He reached the place about three in the afternoon. First, the temple of Trimbakeshwar was visited. This place reminded him of Kedarnath and Badrinath. The plateau on which the town and the temple are built is surrounded on three sides with high mountains. He scaled these mountains one after the other. First to ascend was the small hill of Ambajee. Next the hill of Ganga Dwar. Then the still higher hill, Brahmagiri. The climbing of Brahmagiri was a memorable one. Ramdas went up alone with Ram on his lips. Ascending the top of the hill, he got down the slope. On the other side he came upon a small tank and a *mandir* of Shankar[1] in which there was a sadhu. Ramdas was received by the sadhu very hospitably. He narrated the story of Gautama's *tapasya* on those hills in ancient times. The sadhu lives here alone in the company of a number of monkeys that ran about on the roof of the temple. After sharing with Ramdas his frugal fare, the sadhu pointed to him a thin footpath on the hill which he said would lead him to a place called Jatahshanker.

Accordingly Ramdas started, accompanied also by a *Brahmin* pilgrim. But the *Brahmin* was with him only for a short distance, for when they had to walk amongst brambles and high

---

[1] *Shankar*: Lord Shiva

grown grass and reeds, they missed each other, both having lost their way. Ramdas now found a long line of steps cut into the bosom of the hills. Here he climbed down, and finding below a small opening, crept out of it on the other side and found himself on another hill. Again walking some distance, he came upon another similar passage and going down here as well, he came upon the other side to a different hill. Here again he proceeded further still, now through thorny shrubs and thick growth of reeds. At last he came to the end of the summit. Here appeared on the extreme edge of the slope something like a beaten track.

Now Ramdas was standing on the brow of a tremendous precipice. The bottom of the hill could be seen from this place straight down vertically, many hundreds of feet below. Any attempt to walk upon the slope was a very dangerous experiment. But a strange fascination seemed to have seized Ramdas. He crept slowly upon the slope. His hold was thin dried-up grass that grew on the hill. Both his hands were engaged in this task. He was now on the slope. It was a condition in which every moment had to be counted; but he was careless and fearless. Suddenly, the dried grass in his left hand gave away and his left foot slipped. Ramdas was even now calm and unperturbed—his lips uttering Ram's name aloud.

It was rather a very severe test on Ram's powers of protection. But nothing is impossible for the all-powerful Ram. Ramdas' other hand was then grasping a stone, which was also a little shaky. By a concentration of all strength at this point he recovered his balance and drew up the leg that had slipped. This became all possible by the aid of Ram alone. It was Ram alone who pulled him up. A few minutes later he was again on the same path that led him to the precipice. While returning he came across a small tank full of pure spring water. Here he met again the *Brahmin* pilgrim whom he had missed. Jatahshanker could not be found so both retraced their steps to the *mandir* and finding the way downhill before evening, reached Trimbakeshwar.

That night Ramdas could not help thinking again and again of the wonderful manner in which Ram saved him while he was about to fall down the precipice. That same evening he mounted up a small hillock and spent some time in the *ashram* of a Mahratta[2] saint. During his stay in the *dharmashala*, he had also the unique privilege of having the *darshan* of an old, learned *sannyasi* permanently residing in the *dharmashala*. In the course of his talk with Ramdas the venerable saint condemned, in no uncertain terms, the use of silk by *Brahmins* as a sacred cloth. His contention was that cotton cloth is the best suited and of the purest material since it is made from a plant's flower, whereas silk is produced by destroying thousands of innocent silkworms. So he considered that, instead of silk cloth being holy, it was the most sinful article for wear and must be totally eschewed. Further he said that *crores*[3] of rupees worth of silk was every year being imported from China, Japan and other countries, which meant an enormous drain upon the poor and diminishing wealth and resources of India.

The old saint spoke with great earnestness and asked Ramdas if he agreed with him. Ramdas at once gave his humble and unqualified approval of his diatribe upon the evil. The *sannyasi* was so zealous upon this subject that he was busy circulating notices, getting them pasted on the walls of temples and *dharmashalas*, writing to newspapers and calling upon all devout people to give up once and for all the use of silk which he described as nothing short of a most sinful luxury. He explained that the wearing of silk was unknown to the ancients of India, since no mention of it could be found anywhere in the Vedas, and its use has not been enjoined by any religious authority.

The *sannyasi* was kind to Ramdas and desired that he should remain in Trimbakeshwar for some days more. But Ram's command had already come. So next morning, Ramdas left the place for Panchavati, which he reached in the after-

---
[2] From Maharashtra State
[3] *crore*: 10 million

noon. He visited the Sri Ramachandra *mandir* of Panchavati and had the *darshan* of several sadhus on the banks of the Godavari. The following day, walking up to the railway station, he started by the night train, and travelling via Manmad and Kurduwadi came to Pandharpur.

36.

PANDHARPUR–BIJAPUR

PANDHARPUR VITHOBA[1] is indeed a most popular Deity. He is visited by pilgrims from all parts of India. Hundreds of them are every day coming to Pandharpur with this object. It is said that on important festival days thousands of people are pouring into the place. Here flows the beautiful river Chandrabhaga. A little away from the banks of this river is situated the temple of Vithoba. To go inside this temple is to merge oneself in an atmosphere full of spiritual fervor. On one side, a group is busy performing *bhajan* ringing cymbals; on another side, a saintly figure is preaching the greatness of *bhakti*, giving now and again a sweet song or an apt illustration. Again at another place, some saints with the tambourine in hand are singing *abhangas*[2] of Tukaram. Some are sitting near the massive pillars of the temple deeply absorbed in meditation. Still others are found occupying the verandas reading religious books. Some again are dancing, only repeating Vithal, Vithal! O, it was a scene in which Ramdas lost himself every time he entered the temple. There is always a huge rush of pilgrims for the *darshan* of Vithoba.

Ramdas remained in Pandharpur for five days, occupying a small *mandir* of Shankar on the banks of the holy river, in the company of two sadhus. Ram is very kind. Ramdas here came to know that Mangalvedha lay only 12 miles from Pandharpur.

---
[1] *Vithoba*: Lord Krishna
[2] *abhangas*: devotional songs

One morning he walked this distance and reached Mangalvedha at midday. In the town a kind merchant served him with food. It appeared as though the merchant was looking forward to Ramdas' arrival. Ram's plans are always so when man leaves everything to Him without interference. Mangalvedha is a small town where about 400 years ago the great saint Damaji Pant flourished. The ancient and worn-out fortress in which Damaji was holding office for managing public affairs under the Badshah of Bijapur is still there.

Damaji was a great devotee of Vithoba of Pandharpur. The way how he came to the relief of thousands of starving, famine-stricken fellowmen by a loving and fearless act of charity, and how God Vithoba saved his *bhakta* by assuming the form of a pariah, form the theme of a well-known story in this great saint's life. The memory of the saint is still dear and sacred to everyone of this blessed town even to this day. On the *samadhi* of this saint there is now a temple containing three idols, viz., of Vithoba, Rukhmayi and Damaji. *Bhajan*, *puja* and reading of religious books are going on in this temple throughout the day and a great part of the night. There is also a sadhu residing here. Ramdas remained in the society of the sadhu for five days. They were indeed, by the grace of Ram, very happy days.

The sadhu was a simple and childlike man—a true *shishya*[3] of Damaji. He was rearing a white cow of which he was very fond. He called her Krishnabai. He has written some beautiful verses in Marathi upon the *gomata*[4]. Truly, the cow represents the Mother of the universe and is a grand ideal of all that is gentle, pure, self-sacrificing and innocent. The *gomata* yields milk, out of which curds, butter and ghee are made for the use of man. And again, she is the mother of the bullocks that plough the fields for growing corn that provide food grains for the use of man. Even her dung is of great use as manure and fuel. In Kathiawar, where there are no trees and forests close by, the common fuel is only cow-dung cakes. Then again, after

---
[3] *shishya*: disciple
[4] *gomata*: mother cow

death, various useful articles are made out of her skin and bones. O Mother, thou art indeed *Kamadhenu*[5]!

Ramdas now started by Ram's command on foot for Bijapur which is 40 miles from Mangalvedha. He came across, on the way, a number of villages and in almost all the villages he was welcomed by the resident sadhus of the place. In some places the villagers prevailed upon Ramdas to stay with them for two or three days. So the journey proved, by the grace of Ram, a most delightful one. At last he reached Bijapur in the evening. He went straight to a *Ram–mandir* and receiving some *prasad* after *puja*, took rest for the night in a small shed attached to the temple.

Next morning, Ram prompted him to go about enquiring for any generous-hearted merchant who supplied foodstuffs to sadhus. For every town or city contains such charitable *bhaktas*. Ramdas had given up doing this kind of thing independently; for, in fact, foodstuffs were of no use to him since he did not cook. If food was given, he would take, otherwise not. But in this particular instance, it was all the prompting of Ram. At last, knocking about for 2 or 3 hours from one bazaar to the other, from one lane to the other, from one shop to the other, he was directed to a place where he was given some wheat flour, *dal* and one *anna* for sundries. These things Ramdas tied up in a piece of cloth and was passing in the crowded streets without knowing where to go. When he was in the middle of the street, he was detained by a call from a young man who approached him from a high-storied building.

"Will you deign, Maharaj, to accept *bhiksha* at my house today?" he asked. "If you can do so, you may come to this house at 12 o'clock."

It was then about 10 o'clock. Ramdas accepting the invitation, proceeded onwards and eventually sat down on the outer veranda of a shop which was shut. Ten minutes had not elapsed when he descried at a short distance an old man with

---

[5] *Kamadhenu*: a celestial, wish-granting cow

a rosary of large *rudraksha* around his neck, standing in front of a house for alms in the hot sun. Now Ramdas clapped his hands and beckoned the old *bhikshu* to the place where he was sitting. He came. After mutual salutations, he took his seat beside Ramdas. Ramdas now handed over to him, as prompted by Ram, the bundle containing wheat flour, etc., as also the *anna* piece. No sooner had Ramdas made this offer than he stared at Ramdas with a solemn, uncertain and vacant gaze. Then, falling at the feet of Ramdas and clasping his feet, he looked up and said:

"At last, God has shown Himself to me! You are none else but God to whom I was praying and praying all these years." Then again he cried out, "Am I dreaming or is this a reality?"

Now Ramdas was utterly bewildered and was quite unable to understand the cause of his strange behavior.

"What ails you, O brother?" asked Ramdas.

"The fact is, Maharaj," he replied, "from morning I have been wandering for alms. I could get until now only half an *anna* (here he showed two quarter *anna* pieces). At home there is an old sickly wife, besides two children, to be fed. To go home empty handed means the starvation of these innocent children. I was praying to God in all humility, but I was almost losing hope when you, whom I look upon as God Himself, called me and offered me food."

O Ram, what a deplorable tale! O Ram, how many are there in the world who are always on the verge of starvation! This occurrence is narrated here in detail to show the acuteness of the misery of starvation that exists among the poor, downtrodden lower classes. O rich brothers, O rich mothers, O Ram!

Now parting from the old friend, Ramdas came to the house of the merchant–friend who had invited him. Here both the merchant and his wife treated poor Ramdas most kindly. They pressed him to remain at their house for two days. During this time he visited the vast and imposing pile, the Jumma Masjid; climbed the turret and ascended the gallery of that gigantic structure, Golgumata. The masterly architecture of this building is indeed wonderful. The hollow dome of the building reverberates the slightest sound inside seven times. The sound is also magnified. A man standing near this huge leviathan structure appears like an ant in comparison. Ram showed Ramdas all these marvelous things.

37.

SRI SIDDHARUDHA SWAMI

NOW RAMDAS, catching a train going still southward, reached Hubli at last. The idea of going to Hubli was put into his head by brother Ramakrishna Rao of Bombay, who is a great *bhakta* of the famous saint of Hubli—Sri Siddharudha Swami. Ram took him here to obtain for him the *darshan* of this great sage. It was past midday when he reached the *Mutt* of Sri Siddharudha which is about three miles distant from the railway station. The *Mutt* consisted of three sets of buildings. The first one in the lines was a solid block of granite over which was erected a tall conical *gopura*[1]. This temple was intended to serve as a repository of the remains of the Swami after he had entered *mahasamadhi*. The other two were extensive buildings constructed in such a way as to leave a large square yard in the interior. Of these, the second one was a *dharmashala* wherein reside *sannyasis*, *bhaktas* and pilgrims. Facing the *Mutt* there were two beautiful tanks. On the other side of the tanks there was a grove of trees yielding cool shade. The *Mutt* was situated in very charming and healthy surroundings.

Ramdas, entering the *Mutt*, was through the kindness of friends there, duly introduced to Sri Siddharudha at whose feet he prostrated himself most reverently. Here he spent about 10 days most happily. In the mornings and evenings there were reading and exposition of religious texts. Ramdas

---
[1] *gopura*: a tall tower, often found in Ancient Indian temples

listened to, nay, drank in the words of wisdom that fell from the lips of the learned Sage. Ram had so arranged matters for him that the *upadesh* the Swami gave during those days happened to be just what would lead him further in his spiritual progress. At other times he would wander about in the fields behind the *Mutt* and remain mostly at the tomb or *samadhi* of the late Kabirdas, the great Muslim saint of that place. Ramdas was clearly able to experience a spiritual atmosphere charged with peace and calmness inside the Math and *dharmashala*, especially at the time of the presence of the great Swami. Sri Siddharudha was a great Yogi of an advanced age. He was kind, affable, hospitable and full of tranquility.

Now news reached Mangalore that Ramdas was staying at the *Mutt* at Hubli. His former wife, but present mother (as all women are mothers to Ramdas) and his child came there to fetch him. Sri Siddharudha Swami was appealed to by them in the matter and the kind-hearted saint advised him to go with them to Mangalore. Ramdas submitted to the order, feeling that it came from Ram Himself. Ram always means well and He does everything for the best. The mother (i.e., Ramdas' former wife) proposed to him to return to *samsara*, to which he replied:

"O mother, it is all the work of Ram. Ram alone has freed humble Ramdas from the bonds of *samsaric* life, and he resides now at Ram's holy feet. He is now the slave of Ram and prays to Him always to keep him as such. To trust and acknowledge His supreme powers of protection over all, and believe that He alone is the doer of all actions and possessor of all things is the only way to be rid of the miseries of life. Therefore, O mother, throw off your burden of cares and anxieties and approaching the divine feet of Ram, live there always in peace and happiness. This is all poor Ramdas can ask you to do."

Now, under the kind care and escort of the mother, he started by train and reaching Mormugao embarked upon a steamboat which took them in due course to Mangalore. As the party came up to the *bundar*[2], Ramdas, as bid by Ram, walking in advance, directed his steps straight to the Kadri hills, where he remained for the night. Next day, by Ram's will, he visited the house of brother Sitaram Rao—a brother by the old relation and a great *bhakta* of Ram. A few days later, he had the happiness of the *darshan* of his Gurudev (father by old relationship) who had given him the *upadesh* of the divine *Ram-mantram*. Now, [this was in 1923] Ramdas stays by Ram's command in a cave called "Panch Pandav cave" on the Kadri hill, and lives there a serene life, devoting his whole time in talking about, writing of and meditating on that all-loving and glorious Ram.

Om Sri Ram Jai Ram Jai Jai Ram

---

[2] *bundar*: seaport

Appendices

In The Cave
Heart-pourings when Ramdas resided in the Panch Pandav cave

O Ram, Thou art father, mother, brother, friend, preceptor, knowledge, fame, wealth and all. Sole refuge Thou art, make Thy slave merge always in Thee—in Thee alone.

❖

O Ram, what Thy slave Ramdas should do or should not do must be determined by Thee alone. He is bewildered. He is helpless; make him resign all to Thee. Let him live, move and have his being in Thee. Let him eat, drink, sleep, move, sit, stand, talk, think, look, hear, smell, touch, do everything in Thy name and for Thy sake only. O Ram, O Divine Mother, Ramdas is Thine totally, completely—heart, soul, body, mind, everything, everything.

❖

O Ram, Thy slave cannot know what to think of Thy infinite love. Shall he weep over it? Shall he smile over it? Shall he cry over it? Shall he laugh over it? Thy love is at times so grand, majestic, vast and gushing like the mighty ocean and its roaring waves. At times it is so soft, tender, gentle, silent, like the mild flow of a tiny stream and her musical ripples.

❖

O Ram, keep Thy slave always absorbed in Thee. He is at once Thy slave and Thy child. He is willing to serve Thee in every way according to the wisdom Thou givest him. He is Thy innocent child, looking always for Thy guidance and security. Never allow him to leave Thy holy feet. O Ram, never put him in a situation in which he would forget Thee.

❖

O Ram, O Mother, save, save, save Thy humble slave—Thy ignorant child.

❖

O Love Infinite, infuse into the arid heart of this child at least a small measure of Thy love.

❖

O Ramdas, drink, drink, always the sweet nectar of Ram's love.

❖

O Ram, make Ramdas mad of Thee—mad—mad, stark mad. He wants nothing besides this. Let him talk like a fool only of Thee, O Ram. Let the world declare him a mad man, yes, mad of Thee, Ram.

❖

Ramdas cares not for the opinion of this man or that. He is not to be bound. O Ram, see that he is not bound. Let him be bound only by Thy shackles, those are the shackles of Thy love. But Thy love is free. So where are the shackles? It is an enchanting freedom in fetters. O Ram, the madness of Thy love, how sweet, how intoxicating, how charming!

❖

O Ram, purify the mind of Thy slave. Let him not see evil anywhere. Let him not see faults in others but only good. O Ram, have mercy on Thy slave. Fill his mind with Thy grace. Thou art the sole refuge of Thy slave. O Protector! Loving Parent of the whole universe, lift Thy slave up from the consciousness of a narrow life in a perishable body. Make him realize Thy infinite love. O Ramdas, rise, rise above the narrow limitations of your own making. Ram asks you in all love and kindness: "Speed up my child, come up; here is My hand, grasp it and rise out of the bondage in which you are." O Love, O Life Universal, O Mother, O Ram, how glorious it is always to bask in the sunshine of Thy loving influence!

❖

O Ramdas, you are in Ram and out of Him. You are everywhere along with Him; He is everywhere along with you. He cannot leave you; you cannot leave Him. He is tied to you and you are tied to Him. You are in His custody; He is in your custody. He cannot do without you; you cannot do without Him. He lives in you and you live in Him. Still, you are His slave and He is your protector, O Ram. Thou art two; but Thou art one. The lover and the loved in fast embrace become one. Two become one and one remains everlasting, infinite, eternal Love. O Love, O Ram! Rave on, mind, charged with the madness of Ram's love.

❖

O Ram, destroy Ramdas' desires. Crush them out of him. Take him on and find him eternal abode in Thee. O madness of Ram, O Love, let harshness, wrath and desire leave Ramdas entirely. Pure, pure be his mind by Thy grace. Ram, save him, save him. O Ram, Thou art Love pervading everywhere; Ram, Ram, Ram everywhere; in, out, in all directions, up, below, in the air, trees, earth, water, sky, space, in all, in all is Ram—is Love. O Love, O Ram, let thrill after thrill of the joy of Thy love pass through the soul of Ramdas. O Ram, O Joy, O Love, O Ecstasy, O Madness, O Goodness, no rest, no sleep, no food, no enjoyment but Thy divine love, divine light. O Joy, Ramdas, remain steeped in the nectar of Ram's infinite love. O Light, dazzle on. O flashes of lightning, O Ram's glory—flash on, flash on! O supreme Happiness, O Bliss! O Joy! Come on, O Ram, Ramdas is lost in Thee. Lost, lost—in joy—in bliss untold—indescribable—lost in Thy effulgence—in Thy light—flash—flash—flash—everywhere flash. Love, love, love, everywhere love!

❖

Fame, name, wealth, relations, friends, all—mirage, nothing real, nothing true there. Mind fixed on Ram derives infinite peace, infinite bliss, for Ram is love, Ram is kindness, Ram is joy.

❖

Let the body go, let the mind go. Let the senses disappear. Let the worlds vanish. Let all that appears pass out of their phantom-existence. Ram—the love eternal—the bliss eternal—lives, endures, is pure, undefiled, serene, peaceful. All hail Ram, all hail!

❖

Madness of Ram. Madness of Ram's love. Come on, take possession of Ramdas and make him swim for ever and ever in the ocean of Thy unfathomable love.

❖

Sweet madness, cool madness, mild madness, peace madness, because it is tempered with Ram's elixir of love.

❖

Away all joys of this fleeting world! The sun of Ram's bliss is up, rising in all his glory, shedding resplendent rays of peace and love all around, dispelling the darkness of misery—nay, paling down the very stars and moon—the fading pleasures of a transient world. Away!

❖

The bird has flown away from the cage and is soaring high up in the air, losing itself in the vast space, lost in Ram, a drop in the ocean.

❖

O mind, be always firm and fixed on Ram. Every other occupation for you is utterly useless. In your pursuit after Ram, let no opinion of the world disturb you. When Ram is thine, you do not want anything. Keep Ram's company always. Then your talk, your actions, your thoughts are all His. Ramdas, wake up, shake up, never wax slow in your progress. Go, leap, leap—pluck the golden fruit—enjoy eternal bliss! O, how sweet the fruit—the taste is intoxicating with the soft love of Ram!

❖

You are nothing, Ramdas. You have no worth, Ramdas. If any good comes from you, it is all Ram's. You are only a piece of stinking clay, away with your vanity!

❖

Ramdas, you are now mad, completely mad. O sweet madness, madness, madness! O Love, O Love! Ramdas, you are really mad. Now, Ram is the theme of your madness. You are stark mad, Ramdas. Drink, drink Ram's love, Ram's nectar. Ram's light dazzles everywhere.

❖

Ramdas, you are free, nothing binds you. You are free like air. Soar high and high in the heavens until you spread everywhere and pervade the whole universe. Become one with Ram. All Ram! All Ram! What a grand spectacle to see the dazzling light of Ram everywhere! Flash, Flash, Flash—lightning flashes! O Grandeur! O Divinity, O Love, O Ram! Ramdas, your madness is worth everything that is and that is not in the world. Fling away wisdom, who wants it? Wisdom is poison—madness is nectar—madness of Ram, mind you Ramdas. Ramdas, you have no separate existence. Ramdas, who are you? A phantom of your own creation. Break off and abide in Ram, that ocean of Love, Bliss and Light. "The dew drop slips into the shining sea."

❖

Childlike nature, madness of Ram and supreme wisdom mean one and the same thing.

❖

O Ram, Thy slave Ramdas is Thine completely. His life is totally consecrated to Thy service. Let the sweetness of Thy infinite love enter the soul of Ramdas; give strength to Thy slave to withstand all the temptations of a most unreal world. Let him always live in Thee!

❖

O Ram, Thy slave cries to Thee repeatedly to make him mad of Thee, but Thou dost not listen to his heartfelt prayers. Thou bringest on the madness only for a short time, why not always? Let his mind think on nothing else but Thee, Thee and Thee alone—that is the madness he craves for. Have pity on him!

✦

Let Ramdas' mind be filled with Thee when awake, in sleep, in dreams. O Ram, O Mother, O Protector, have mercy on Thy child and Thy slave!

✦

Start Ramdas on his mission—O Ram! Let him go out into the world, toil, suffer, die for Thy sake. Let him face contempt, persecution, nay, death for Thy rule of Love, Bliss and Light. In the fire of this ordeal, let Ramdas purify his lethargic soul. Height of misery is height of happiness. To rise above both is true bliss—true peace. O Ram, give the call! Let Thy stern command come. If not, make this body—worthless stuff—wither and perish. Let every minute of its existence be utilized for Thy service, Ram.

✦

The lull has passed. The storm is ahead. Ramdas feels waves on waves rising in him, mighty waves of a surging ocean. O Ram, guard Thy slave, give him energy, give him strength—give him Thy wisdom, and make him sacrifice himself at the altar of Truth, at the shrine of Love, in the flame of Light. All Ram, Ram, Ram, Ram! O save, save, save! Ramdas is Thine, life, body, soul, all, all!

✦

Make Ramdas mad of Thee. Quick—no time to lose. Quick! Quick! Have mercy on him. Om Sriram!

✦

Rise, rise, O despair of hope! Rise, rise, O joyous misery! Rise, rise, O light of darkness! O Rise, rise, lovely dream of an eternal life! Rise, rise O Bliss, Grandeur—what indescribable happiness to cry, to weep, to smile, to laugh, to live, to die for Ram's love, Ram's grace, Ram's light! Om Sriram!

Peace, Peace, Peace!
Ram, Ram, Ram!

❖

You are not weak, Ramdas, you are all-powerful. Ram has infused into you His divine effulgence. You are the infinite seed. Ram has thrown a flood of light into you. Wake up! You are strong, you can conquer everything by the power of Ram's love. Don't grovel, don't feel weak. From hilltops, from housetops, sound the trumpet of Ram's glory, Ram's love. Be bold, forward—march! Brave the storm. Destiny is your slave. Keep her under foot. What fear have you when Ram is your ally? Leave off narrow limitations. Rise and soar and grasp the whole globe in one embrace of love. Your dwelling place is the whole universe which is your body. You live in it as love. There is nought but love, love supreme. Every leaf, every blade of grass, every particle of dust, every tiniest life sings aloud of Thy love, O Ram. Every moonbeam, every sun's ray, every twinkle of the stars radiates Thy love, O Ram. Every tear, every smile, every ripple, every sweet whisper of joy is pregnant with Thy love, O Ram!

❖

O Ramdas, rise to the very height of renunciation and there sit on its crest and view the transient nature of the whole show around you. Everywhere you see, birth, growth, death. All, all are running finally along the same road to destruction. What a terrible state of despair would have faced man in the midst of this vast cremation ground—this vast graveyard where all objects are ultimately reduced to dust and ashes—had there not been that sweet and eternal influence, that divine ambrosia called Love, which is a veritable lustrous reality that runs through the vanishing forms that make up this wild, varied and grand structure of the universe. Love is Happiness. Love is God. Love is Ram.

❖

O Ram! Fill, fill, fill, Ramdas with Thy nectar-like love. Let no thought of evil, no thought of difference cross his mind. Make him look upon all with the light of Love.

❖

O Ram! It is Thou that weepest in the sorrows of the world. It is Thou that smilest in the happiness of the world. Still Thou art above all happiness and above all sorrow.

❖

Ram! Thou art an eternal lovebaby. Ramdas is ever bent upon catching Thy tender smiles, but they elude his grasp.

❖

Love sheds her cooling light. Ramdas opens his lips to drink of it, but the light slips away.

❖

Ramdas at last catches the smiles—so many lustrous nothings that beam upon his face.

❖

Ramdas at last drinks deep the light of love and softly floats upon the sea of peace.

❖

O Love, O Ram, envelop everything in the soft glare of Thy radiance. O Love, let all vibrations be rhythmical and true. Let the inexpressible sweetness of bliss reign everywhere.

❖

O Ram, make Ramdas mad of Thee. Let him not talk of anything else but Thee. Let him think of nothing else but Thee. Thou art so merciful, Thou art so loving. O Love, O Mercy, make Ramdas completely Thine!

❖

Whatever Thou dost Ram, Thou dost for the best; Ramdas is entirely Thine. Thou dost make him walk, talk, think, act, all as Thou wilt. He has not to feel sorry or regret for anything. He dwells in Thee always. He can see Thee, Ram, everywhere. Thou alone hast taken the form of this universe—this vast, picturesque, varied group of worlds. O, what a grand display is Thine! O, what a sublime manifestation! The vast sheets of water—the mighty oceans that dazzle in the sunlight like molten silver—bearing in their bosom a variety of animal lives of their own creation—art Thyself. O extensive sky, what a magnificent structure is Thine! A limitless blue dome pictured here and there with fantastic shaped white fleecy clouds, sustaining in her mighty embrace innumerable creatures of her own making. O Earth, whose unseen circumference vainly attempts to measure the bounds of the sky that appears to clasp Thee! What an indescribable scene Thou dost present to the wondrous gaze of the sun, moon and stars that are never tired of viewing Thy beauties at ever changing altitudes. Thy valleys are full of green verdure—sparkling water running through them all. Thy high mountains are shooting up into the sky—those gigantic guardians of Thy peace. The widespread forests, green and yellow-hued form Thy beautiful garment, in the loving folds of which Thou bringest into being untold variety of lives.

❖

Who brought this gorgeous show into being? It is all the work of Ram—the work of Love—Ram himself manifested in all His grandeur of love.

❖

O Ramdas, you have nothing in the world to call your own. All belong to Ram, including yourself. Ram does everything for the best. Ram is the doer. Ramdas, live always in tune with Him. O Ram, see that this prayer is granted. Thou art all in all to Thy slave. He wants Thee and nothing else. O Ram, purify Ramdas' mind. Let no evil thought enter there.

❖

O Ram, Thou art everywhere,
   O Ramdas, thou art nowhere

O Ram, Thy will alone is supreme.
O Ramdas, thou hast no will.
O Ram, Thou art the only reality.
O Ramdas, thou hast no existence.
O Ram, O infinite Love, let Ramdas lose himself in Thee.

❖

O Ram, Thy Love pervades everywhere. Thy Light shines everywhere. Thy Bliss absorbs everything. Ram, Thou art Light, Love and Bliss. Ramdas, thou livest in this Light, in this Love, in this Bliss. Ramdas, thou hast no separate existence. Thou art free, as free as Love, as free as Light, as free as Bliss. Love all, shed Light on all, share Bliss with all. Thou art all and all Thyself. Thou and all make Ram, that glorious Ram. Ram is one. Ram appears as many. One is real. Many is false. One—One everywhere, and that is Ram. Ramdas, thy will is the will of Ram. Live only for the sake of Ram. Ram has made you mad of Him. Blessed are you, Ramdas, Ram's madness means everything for you, for that matter—means everything for everybody. In this madness there is no pain, no perplexity, no ignorance, no weakness, no sorrow, no hate, no evil of any kind. It is purely made up of Love, Light, Bliss, Strength, Power, Wisdom, every good of every kind.

❖

Ramdas, all praise, all honor, all respect is for Ram, because your speech, your act, your thought is all in the name of Ram—for the sake of Ram—prompted by Ram—acted by Ram—thought by Ram—listened to by Ram. All in Ram, by Ram, through Ram, on Ram, about Ram, for Ram. All Ram, Ram, nothing but Ram! Om Sri Ram! Om, Om, Om! Ram, Ram, Ram! This is madness of Ram. It is a grand madness—Blissful, Lightful, Loveful, Ramful. No thought but of Ram. No work but of Ram. No talk but of Ram. Talk in Ram, work in Ram, thought in Ram, silence in Ram, sleep in Ram, dream in Ram. Ram is in everything. Everything is in Ram. Ram is in everything. Everything is Ram. Om Sriram!

❖

Ram is form, Ram has assumed form. Ram is with form. Ram is without form. Ram is being. Ram is non-being. Ram appears, Ram disappears. Ram knows. Ram knows not. Love and hate is in Ram. Light and darkness is in Ram. Bliss and pain is in Ram. Wisdom and madness is in Ram. Strength and weakness is in Ram. Still Ram is beyond all these, free from Love and hate, Light and darkness, Bliss and pain, Wisdom and madness, Strength and weakness. Om, Om, Om! Ram, Ram, Ram! Peace, Peace, Peace! O Ram, Thou art the point where Love and hate meet, Light and darkness meet, Bliss and pain meet, Wisdom and madness meet, Strength and weakness meet. Om Sriram—Thou art Peace, stillness—unchangeable, unshakable, eternal, infinite—all powerful, inconceivable, incomprehensible. Om, Om, Om!

❖

There are two ladders, Love and hate, projecting from Thee. O Ram. To reach Thee, i.e., to climb up, the ladder of Love is used. To quit Thee, i.e., to climb down, the ladder of hate is used. Love leads to unity. Hate leads to diversity. Unity is happiness. Diversity is misery. Therefore, O Ramdas, select the upward course of Love that takes you to ultimate Peace—everlasting and eternal—which is Ram. When you quit Ram, hate leads you down to where you sink into pain, fear and death. Om Sriram!

❖

Ramdas, don't be proud. Consider that none is inferior to you in the world. All deserve to be treated with respect and love.

❖

Let your mind, O Ramdas, turn always the *chakra* [wheel] of *Ramsmaran* [remembrance of God] and in due course you will make the mind wear the white *khaddar* of Purity.

❖

O Ram, Ramdas is Thy slave, Thy entire slave. He implores Thee to strictly watch every act he performs, every word that falls from his lips and every thought that comes into this mind. O Ram, see that nothing unworthy of Thee or unacceptable to Thee be done, talked or thought of by Thy slave. Let Ramdas' actions be always right and good. Let his speech be always wise and gentle. Let his thoughts be always holy and pure. In short, let Ramdas' acts, words and thoughts emanate directly from the meditation of Thy Divine Self. Om Sriram!

❖

O Ram, what a glorious being Thou art. Ramdas lays his head at Thy holy feet. Deign to shed Thy full lustre on Thy slave. Make him Thine, Thine totally. Ramdas has no refuge but Thee—no parent but Thee—no guide but Thee, no master but Thee, no higher ideal than Thee. Have mercy on him, O Ram, have mercy. Above all, O Ram, see that he does not forget Thee. To forget Thee means for him utter ruin. Ramdas cannot bear the very thought of it. O Ram, Ramdas has full trust in Thee. He knows that what Ramdas begs, Thou grantest at once. Let him always live in Thee, in Thee alone. Om Sriram!

❖

O Ram, save, save Thy child, Thy slave. Let every fibre of his being thrill to the music of Thy madness; the very blood of his veins rush impelled by the fury of Thy madness; his very bones tatter and shatter in their seats by the repeated blows inflicted by Thy madness; his whole frame quiver, tremble and shake by letting fall on him an avalanche of Thy madness. Om Sriram!

❖

Rise, rise, O Ramdas, fly above all, soar in the heavens, mingle in the flood of light poured down by the glorious sun. Let the pure, rarefied air above encircle you all round. Let space itself swallow you up. Where are you then, Ramdas? Ramdas is nowhere. Ramdas is now mere madness, an airy nothing. Truth, the Great Truth, Ram, hath devoured you—and you are no more, no more, no more! Om Sriram!

❖

O Ramdas, become one with the greenness of the leaves. Be absorbed in the splendor of light. Mix with the mists of the hills. Be the breath of the wind, the blue of the sky, the golden hues of the dawn, the stillness of the night. Om Sriram!

❖

O Ram, Thou art kindness. Thou art love. Thou art the great Truth. Let Ramdas cling to Thee fast. Let him not lose his hold on Thee. Let him always clasp Thee firmly. Let him always live with Thee in Thee. Let him not be separated from Thee. Let him always remain in Thy embrace. O Ram, enfold Thy slave always in Thy arms and never let him go. Make him fearless, bold and firm—firm in his vows—firm in his faith in Thee. Let contact with the world not affect him. Ramdas, always remember that you are alone in the world in the company of Ram.

❖

Ramdas, in spite of Ram's unbounded grace upon you, you are still weak. Ramdas, you are still small and insignificant—full of imperfections—full of defects. Cry, cry; weep, weep. O Ramdas, cry and weep. Take off, O Ram, all his egoism.

❖

O Ram, raise a great conflagration—a mighty deluge of fire—and burn up in its devouring flames all the evils that are in Ramdas. The fire is lit, the flames are rising—red tongues of flame—waving, hissing and dancing. Throw in now—by Ram's command—O Ramdas, first, *ahankar* [ego], then *kama* [lust], *krodha* [anger], *lobha* [greed], *moha* [delusion], *mada* [arrogance], *matsarya* [jealousy] in quick succession. Right, they are now all in. Fan the flames, O Ram. All the evils are burning, burning, burning. Now they fly as smoke. Now they fall as ashes. All glory to Thee, O Ram! Now the fire ceases and then a calm prevails—stillness of heavenly repose, filled with the enchantment of Love and Peace, filled with the sweetness of Ram. Freedom, Freedom, O Freedom, *Mukti* [spiritual freedom] is Thy name. Om Sriram!

❖

O Ram, Thy slave is under Thy protection completely. Thou art his sole refuge. He looks to Thee for everything. At all times let Thy sweet name be in his thoughts. O Ram, purify Ramdas' mind, purge it off from all evil and unworthy thoughts. O Ram, Ramdas is Thine. Bear in mind, Ramdas, you live only for Ram. You do not live for anything else, or for anybody else. Ram is the end and aim of your existence. Your very life is bound up with Ram. O Ram, make Ramdas' faith in Thee ever unshakable, ever firm, permanently fixed. Let all Ramdas' thoughts, acts and words proceed directly from Thee—at Thy bidding—in Thy name and for Thy sake only. Let Ramdas' personality merge itself in Thee. Make him Thy abode—or make Thee his abode, one in the other always intermingled. Let there not be a moment's separation—blended, welded together for ever and for ever. Powerful as Thou art, O Ram, Love as Thou art, Light as Thou art, Bliss as Thou art, the great and only Truth as Thou art, Thy slave prays to Thee, begs Thee, implores Thee, cries to Thee, weeps to Thee, prostrates before Thee—O Ram, have pity on Thy slave, make him Thine altogether. Ram, bless, bless Thy slave. To bless Thy slave is to bless the world. To love Thy slave is to love the world. O Ram, O Love infinite, enter into the very being of Ramdas and live there and spread Thy Light, Love and Bliss. Om Sriram.

❖

O Ram, there is a dawn—a brilliant dawn in the heart of Ramdas. There is in it a flood of Light—a flash of Love—a rush of Bliss. Purity dwells where Ram is. He enters—all evils flee. The sun rises, all darkness vanishes. O Ram, how glorious Thou art! The moment Thou art appealed to—Thou listeneth and granteth. O Mother, how kind of Thee. How beautiful is Thy Love, how tender, how soft, how gracious, how true, how bracing, how cooling, how good, O how lasting! O Ram, Thine, Thine is Thy slave—Thine—Thine is this Thy child for ever, for ever, for ever. Om, Om, Om Sriram!

❖

Higher and higher the thought rises until it is lost in the incomprehensible. Deeper and deeper the thought runs down until it is lost in the unfathomable. Wider and wider the thought spreads out until it is lost in the unexplorable. Narrower and narrower the thought contracts until it is lost in the unthinkable. Om Sriram!

❖

Love expands the heart and hate contracts it. There is nothing sweeter than Love. There is nothing more bitter than hate. Love is natural. Hate is unnatural. Love makes and hate destroys. Love is a charming and cooling landscape. Hate is an arid and cheerless desert. Love is harmony. Hate is chaos. Love is light. Hate is darkness. Love is bliss. Hate is misery. Love is life. Hate is death. Love is purity. Hate is impurity. Love combines. Hate breaks up. Love is beauty. Hate is ugliness. Love is health. Hate is disease. Love is sweet music. Hate is discordant noise. Love is wisdom. Hate is ignorance. Love is activity. Hate is dullness. Love is heaven. Hate is hell. Love is God. Hate is illusion. Om Sriram!

❖

O man,
    Where is sweetness—it is in thee
    Where is bitterness—it is in thee
    Where is happiness—it is in thee
    Where is misery—it is in thee

Where is light—it is in thee
Where is darkness—it is in thee
Where is love—it is in thee
Where is hate—it is in thee
Where is heat—it is in thee
Where is cold—it is in thee
Where is good—it is in thee
Where is evil—it is in thee
Where is truth—it is in thee
Where is untruth—it is in thee
Where is wisdom—it is in thee
Where is ignorance—it is in thee
Where is heaven—it is in thee
Where is hell—it is in thee
Where is God—it is in thee
Where is illusion—it is in thee. Om Sriram!

❖

Ram is a reservoir of nectar composed of Light, Love and Bliss. O Ramdas, dive into this well of ambrosia—sink, swim, dance, nay drown thyself in it. Om Sriram!

❖

Ram is a volume of fragrance made up of Light, Love and Bliss. O Ramdas, merge into this wave of aroma; dive, play, gambol—nay, lose thyself in it. Om Sriram!

❖

Ram is a rainbow of colors formed of Light, Love and Bliss. O Ramdas, gaze into this heaven of tints; link, soak, blend—nay, feel thyself one with it. Om Sriram!

❖

Ram is a music of tunes filled with Light, Love and Bliss. O Ramdas, drink at this fountain of thrills; reel, shake, wake—nay, die in the intoxication of it. Om Sriram!

POEMS

OM SRIRAM

> Love softly laid her head,
> Light nimbly danced around,
> Bliss made a joyous sound,
> Peace comes to bless them all.
>
> Love gently oped her eyes,
> Light slowly waved the fan,
> Bliss leapt and flit and ran,
> Peace smiles upon them all.
>
> Love sang her sweetest song,
> Light tuned her charming rays,
> Bliss laughs and rings and plays,
> Peace smiles over them all.
>
> Ram—the blithesome love,
> Ram—the shining light,
> Ram—the blissful height,
> Ram—the peace over all.

THE SOLE REFUGE

> O Ram, I take refuge in Thee,
> Thou art my love, my life, my lead,
> I am in Thee, Thou art in me,
> Thou art my father, mother, indeed.

Thou art the life that pervades all.
In Thee all things and lives reside,
Thou art the life in great and small,
In Thee my friend and brother abide.

Thy lotus feet my constant thought,
Thy light divine my only dream,
To serve Thee is my pleasing lot,
Thou art my wealth, name and fame.

O Ram, how charming is that sound,
O lips, utter Ram Ram,
O mind, meditate Ram Ram,
Forget thyself in Him—in Him.

RAM

O Ram, I see Thy form on every side;
In all the worlds Thy light and glory abide.
O Ram, Thou art the sun that shines on high;
Thou art the moon and stars that deck the sky.

O Ram, Thou art the life that fills all space,
And sets the whirling universe in its race.
O Ram, I see in hills Thy form divine,
In waters vast that flow and wave and shine.

O Ram, I see Thy light in jungles wild,
In trees and plants and verdure mild.
O Ram, all life reflects Thy godly light,
Thou art all in all—Love, Bliss and Might.

OM

The following letter was written by Swami Ramdas to his Gurudev, his brother in his old life, describing his experiences as a travelling pilgrim.

KATOSAN
1923

To Gurudev

Om Sri Ram Jai Ram Jai Jai Ram

Guru Maharaj,
A thousand salutations at thy holy feet. Sri Ram's kindness to me has been so great that after freeing me from the toils of *Samsara*, He has taken me completely under His Divine guidance and support. O! Ram, Thou art my sole refuge. Thou hast been treating me as Thy helpless child ever taking tender care of me. Glory to Thee, O! Ram. Thy kindness and love is infinite. May I be never tired of uttering Thy sweet name, sweeter than nectar. My heart is full with the joy which Sri Ram gives me and I must talk of Him and His love, to whom? O! Ram, to whom? To thee my brother, my Satguru.

Sri Ram is showing me all the wonders of His *Maya*. Sri Ram took me round all the sacred shrines from the south of India to the uttermost north. He guided the footsteps of His humble servant over the blessed Himalayas. The very air over there breathes Sri Ram's Divine presence. The never ending chains of mountains clothed with thick forests are eternal witnesses of Ram's greatness. The Holy Ganga flowing down these hills—giving life and sustenance to millions is singing Ram's glory. Indeed my sight was blessed with enchanting scenes and landscapes—that kept me spellbound. O! Ram, Thou art Grand!

Four hundred miles I walked over the mountains and I never felt any fatigue because Sri Ram was kind to me. He gave me strength and peace. At certain places the ascents were so steep and path so rugged and narrow that a slight slip would pull a man down headlong into the bosom of Ganga hundreds of feet below. When Sri Ram was my guide, what fear have I?

He took me up and up and I walked on fearlessly in full joy chanting His sweet name. Kedarnath was the first place Sri Ram made me visit—about 160 miles from Hardwar. The path to Kedarnath is really dangerous. Many pilgrims have slipped down from the rocks and have been washed away in the torrents of Ganga. Mandakini, a tributary of the Ganges, starts from Kedarnath. The place is covered with snow and cold here is extreme. While ascending to Kedarnath one has to tread upon snow. Who protected me from cold? O! It is Thou. A temple is founded here surrounded on all sides by high rocks fully covered with snow. I ascended one of these rocks which none venture. I first thought it was not so high. I crawled up two hours (nearly), still I could not reach the top. My hold while ascending was rough grass that peeps here and there through snow. It took me nearly 3 hours to travel up to the top of the rock. The distance traversed might be about a mile. To ascend was difficult enough but to descend was extremely perilous. I had simply to slip down 2 or 3 yards at a time and then grip the grass. Further it began to rain not water but big white globules of snow. O! Ram, who protected me here again—it is Thou and Thou alone. After nearly five hours I reached the bottom of the rock. I went to the source of the river Mandakini where the snow melts and flows down. Here I bathed in the ice cold water.

O! Ram, it is by Thy grace I could do all these things. All glory to Thee. I stayed in Kedarnath for one day, then coming down about 40 miles ascended again another chain of hills, the path here was not so bad as the one leading to Kedarnath. But I had to walk over snow at several places and to cover a distance of about 81 miles (milestones are on the way) in order to reach the source of the river Alaknanda, another tributary of the Ganges. This place is called Badrinath or Badrinarayan. Here also the cold is very great. There is a wonder here. From one of the rocks surrounding the temple of Narayan flows down hot fuming water which is collected in a tank in which pilgrims bathe. I remained here also for a day and then came down. Thousands of pilgrims are every year ascending these hills for the *Darshan* of Kedarnath and Badrinath.

Through over exertion many old men and women give up their bodies on the way. Ram's kindness to me during this journey was so great, that I never felt hungry on the way. The pilgrims here were very kind to me. They used to vie with each other in serving my wants which consisted of 2 or 3 *rotis* [flat bread] without salt and boiled potatoes. Some veritably worshipped Ram's humble *das*. Hardwar is the starting point for this Himalayan pilgrimage. About 15 miles up the hills is situated the place called Rishikesh, where about a hundred *Mahatmas* reside in their respective *Ashrams*, thatched huts on the bank of the Ganges. The place is simply enchanting—for a time I thought of settling down here once for all, even without proceeding further on the hills. Even now I wish Sri Ram should take me to this place again so that I might spend the rest of my life in the company of these *sannyasis*, but I do not know what His wish is.

I remained in Rishikesh for 3 days. In my wanderings on the hills, I visited the *Ashrams* of Agastyamuni, Narad and Pandavas [ancients mentioned in the Hindu epics]. It took me 40 days to complete this pilgrimage. These mountains are peopled by hill tribes who live by cultivation. They are so simple and so pure, uncontaminated by the touch of modern civilization. Ramnam is on the lips of all of them. They are a fair complexioned race, clad in clothing made of thick blankets. Even women use thick rugs for *sarees*. They are also rearing cattle and sheep; the latter yield wool which they spin and weave into blankets for their clothing. Wonderful are Thy works O! Ram.

Returning from the Himalayas, Ram directed me towards Mathura, the birthplace of that love incarnate Bhagwan Shri Krishna, wherefrom I visited Gokul, Govardhan and Brindaban. I spent about 10 days on the banks of the holy Jamuna in Brindaban. Brindaban is a delightful place. From Mathura, Sri Ram made me travel down to Raipur, Ajmere (where I visited Khaja Pir, a famous Shrine of Mohammedans) and thence ascended the hill of Pushkar Raj, remained there for 5 days. Then came down further this side. Ram wants me shortly to visit Dwarka and Girnar. Girnar is the stand or seat of Dattattray. After visiting these places and Pandharpur, Ram seems to be wishing to close my itinerant life.

At present I am staying in the *Ashram* of a *Mahatma* of Gujarat. This *Ashram* is situated in a jungle, quite solitary where I can perform *Ram-bhajan* with great pleasure. I am praying Ram to point out and lead me to a place where I can spend the remainder of my life in meditation of Him, in uttering His sweet name. The charming music of the sound, Ram, has sustained me all along and will certainly fill me with His grace till the end. But what He intends to make of me is not known yet.

My prostrations at the holy feet of my Gurudev, our father who gave me that Divine *Ram–mantram* and at thy feet also, I crave for thy blessings. May Sri Ram keep you all blessed with His grace is the fervent prayer of His humble Ramdas. I may by Ram's will remain about 10 days before going to Dwarka.

Love and Namaskars,

RAMDAS

The following letter was written on the eve of Swami Ramdas' departure from Mangalore, by Vittal Rao, the future Swami Ramdas, to Rukmabai, his wife in his pre–pilgrimage life. He mentions Rame, his daughter.

To: Srimathi Rukmabai

Dear Sister,

You are to me only a sister in future. Sriram at whose feet I have surrendered myself entirely has called me away from the past sphere of my life. I go forth a beggar in the wide world chanting the sweet name of Sriram. You know I have no ambition in life except to struggle for the attainment of Sriram's Grace and Love. To that aim alone I dedicate the rest of my life and suffer for it—suffer to any extent. We may not meet again—at least as husband and wife. Walk always in the path of God and truth and make Rame do the same.

Don't give up the spinning wheel. It will give you peace and happiness. Let Rame also work it.

Sriram's blessings on you and Rame—He protects you both.

Yours affectionately,

P. Vittal Rao
12/27/22

Dear Sister,

You are to me only a sister in future. Swami at whose feet I have surrendered myself entirely has called me away from the past sphere of my life. I go forth a beggar in the wide world chanting the sweet name of Swami. You know I have no ambition in life except to struggle for the attainment of Swami's Grace and Love. To that aim alone I dedicate the rest of my life and suffer for it — suffer to any extent. We may not meet again — at least as husband and wife. Walk always in the path of God and Truth and make Renuka do the same.

Don't give up the spinning wheel. It will give you peace and happiness. Let Renuka also work it.

Swami's blessings on you and Renuka — He protect you both.

Yours affectionately,
P. Villookew
27.12.32

Glossary

abhanga – devotional song
Agastyamuni – a sage of great power mentioned in the Hindu epics
ahankar – ego
akhada – monastery, ashram
anna – 1/16th of a rupee (before India went to metric system)
annakshetra – place that offers free food to pilgrims
Arya Samaj – Hindu reform movement started in the 19th century
asan – seat or mat, usually for doing meditation or hatha yoga position, also hatha yoga postures
ashram – a religious center something like a monastery, often started by or dedicated to a saint
avatar – divine incarnation
bairagi – one who is possessed of detachment, a world renouncer (sometimes spelled vairagi)
Balaji – Venkateshwara, a form of Vishnu
Bengali – a person from the state of Bengal
Bhagavad Gita – literally "Song of God," a major Hindu scripture, a chapter from the Hindu epic Mahabharata, that contains Krishna's teachings on realizing God
bhajan – devotional singing
bhaji – a vegetable curry
bhakta – one who is devoted to God
bhakti – devotion to God
bhiksha – alms

Brahma – God in the aspect of creator of the universe, one of the Hindu trinity (see slso Vishnu, Shiva)

Brahman – the Supreme Reality, described in the Upanishads as the absolute Being that supports and pervades the universe

Brahmin – a member of the highest caste, traditionally associated with the occupations of scholar-teacher and priest (sometimes spelled *Brahmana*)

bundar – seaport

chakra – literally "wheel," one of the seven spiritual centers in the body

chandan – paste made from the wood of the sandal tree, said to have a cooling effect

chela – disciple

chits – vouchers

dal – pureed lentils or other legumes

darshan – literally, "vision," the blessing of seeing and being in the presence of a saintly person, holy object or place

das – servant, often in the sense of a servant of God

Dayananda Saraswati – a Hindu reformer and revivalist of the 19th century, founded Arya Samaj

dharmashala – way station for pilgrims

dhed – an untouchable whose job is to clean latrines

doli – cradle-like conveyance

ektar – one stringed instrument

fakir – ascetic or mendicant, often Muslim

furlong – a measure of distance, about 200 yards

gadi – seat made of cotton matting

gerrua – red ochre, used by sannyasis for dyeing their robes orange, to Hindus the color emblematic of renunciation

gomata – literally "mother cow," reflects the high regard Hindus have for cows

gopura – tall towers often found in Indian temples, especially ancient ones

grihastha – householder, a married person

grihasthashram – one of the four stages of life of a Hindu, the householder period, the others being student, retiree

Glossary ♦ 163

and renunciant

guru – spiritual preceptor

Gurudev – literally "Divine Preceptor," a term used by Hindus to refer to and directly address their spiritual teachers, signifying both respect and affection

gurustan – abode of the guru

Hanuman – character in the *Ramayana*, he is considered an embodiment of pure devotion to God, a monkey who helped Lord Ramachandra to rescue his wife Sita

Indra – the king of the gods in the Hindu pantheon

jatah – tuft of matted hair, commonly worn by certain types of Indian ascetics

Kali – the aspect of God as the Divine Mother, Primal Energy, who incarnated as Radha, Sita and various others

kama – sensual pleasure, sometimes used in the sense of lust

kamandhenu – a mythical cow that grants every desire

kamandal – water vessel carried by pilgrims

kambal – blanket

kaupin – loin cloth

khaddar – homespun cloth, the use of which was advocated by Mahatma Gandhi

krodha – anger

kshetra – here, a place that offers free food to pilgrims, also means "place" or "field"

kund – small body of water, typically a "tank" or artificially constructed pond, situated near a temple or holy place

ladoo – sweatmeat balls, a confection

lobha – greed

lota – water container carried by pilgrims

mada – arrogance

Mahabharata – one of two greatest Indian epics, the story of Lord Krishna and the heroic Pandava brothers, of which the Bhagavad Gita forms a chapter

Mahadev – a name of Lord Shiva

mahant – head of a religious institution

mahasamadhi – literally "great absorption (samadhi)," a

saint's final "absorption" into God at the time of his or her physical death

mahatma – great soul

mandap – a decorated structure for seating the image of Divinity or an honored person

mandir – Hindu temple

mantram – sacred verbal formula that is repeated with reverence for its spiritually uplifting and purifying effect

masjid – mosque

matsarya – jealously

math – a religious center, an ashram or monastery

maya – the divine power of illusion that projects the world of multiplicity and conceals the transcendent unity

moha – delusion

mridang – a kind of drum

mukti – spiritual emancipation

mutt – monastery

namaskar – salutation, literally "I bow to God in you"

namaz – prayers to God made by Muslims five times daily

Narad – an enlightened sage believed by Hindus to eternally roam at will between the world of humans and the world of the gods, functioning as a kind of messenger

neem – an Indian tree with bitter tasting leaves but possessing salubrious qualities

panchavati – a holy configuration of five particular kinds of trees used for meditation and other religious functions

panda – the name for Brahmins in Kashmir and certain other North Indian areas

Pandavas – five sons of Pandu who were the heroes of the great Hindu epic, the *Mahabharata*

pies – (singular "pie" or "pice") 1/64th of a rupee or 1/4 of an anna (used before the metric system came to India)

plantain – a type of large banana

pranava – the seminal sound of the universe: OM

prasad – food eaten after it has first been offered to God or a saint

puja – worship
pujari – temple priest
puri – a kind of unleavened flat bread, deep fried
Ram Japa – repetition of a name of God
Ram-bhajan – devotional singing
Ram-smaran – remembrance of God
Rama Tirtha – a highly respected Hindu saint who lived around the turn of the century
Ramachandra – considered by Hindus to be an incarnation of God, the hero of the *Ramayana*
Ramayana – one of the two greatest Indian epics, the story of Sita and Lord Ramachandra
rishis – ancient sages of India, to whom were revealed the vedas (scriptures)
roti – a kind of flat bread, a chapati
rupee – the Indian national currency
rudraksh – (or rudraksha) a round seed that is sacred to Lord Shiva, used in rosaries by devotees of God in that form
sadavart – food given free to wandering monks
sadhana – spiritual practices and disciplines
sadhu – travelling homeless monk
sadhu-Ram – the name Swami Ramdas gives to the sadhus who travel with him, literally "God in the form of sadhu"
samadhi – a state of complete "absorption" in spiritual consciousness, also used to designate the tomb of a saint, as the place of his or her final "absorption" in the infinite. See *mahasamadhi*
samsara – the phenomenal world in which the soul is bound in cycles of birth and rebirth, the "worldly life"
samsaric – worldly, pertaining to the illusions, desires and bondage of worldly life
sandhya – the three "junction" periods—dawn, noon and twilight—at which observant Hindus are expected to recite special prayers
sannyasin – religious mendicant
sannyasini – female sannyasin

sati – self-immolation by a woman on the funeral pyre of her husband, practiced historically by certain upper-caste groups in certain parts of India. Now illegal.
satsang – fellowship of devotees of God or of a saint
seth – merchant
sethu – (or setu) a bridge, Lord Ramachandra's bridge between India and Lanka, as related in the Hindu epic, the *Ramayana*
Shankar – a name of Lord Shiva
shishya – disciple
Shiva-ling – symbol of Lord Shiva
Shiva – (sometimes spelled Siva) God in the aspect of destroyer, one of the Hindu trinity (see also Brahma, Vishnu)
Shivaratri – an annual event in February or March of special worship of Shiva throughout the night
shuddhi – literally "purification," refers to the movement which promoted reconversion back to Hinduism
Sita – an incarnation of the Divine Mother, wife of Lord Ramachandra (the unmanifest aspect of God) whose story is told in the epic Ramayana
sloka – a verse, usually of scripture
tabooth – altar used in Muslim worship
tank – pond, often man made
tapasya – spiritual austerities
toddy – country palm liquor
Tulsidas – author of the popular version of the Ramayana, lived in the 1500's, revered throughout Hindi speaking India
upadesh – initiation or instruction from a guru
vakil – lawyer
Vishnu – God in the aspect of the maintainer of the universe, one of the Hindu trinity (see also Brahma, Shiva)

UPCOMING BOOKS FROM BLUE DOVE PRESS:
expected date of publication in parentheses

In the Vision of God – volumes I & II
by Swami Ramdas (October 1994)

These two books conclude the trilogy of Swami Ramdas that started with *In Quest of God*. They continue an account of his pilgrimage across the length and breadth of India, as a penniless pilgrim. Witty yet inspiringly and compellingly told.

Saint Teresa of Avila — A Biography
by William Thomas Walsh (March 1995)

This book is considered by some the best English language biography of this great saint. It is charmingly written, with great insight into the spiritual life. Walsh is devoted to her, yet does not shrink from reporting the strange and unusual events in her life that for him only add to the compellingness of her witness. This book is a complete and well researched look into the life of a very remarkable saint.

The Ultimate Medicine
by Sri Nisargadatta Maharaj, edited by Robert Powell (October 1994)

Born in 1897, Nisargadatta Maharaj spent his early years on his family's small farm in rural India. At age 34 he met his guru and three years later he realized the ultimate Self. In the tradition of the Sage Ramana Maharshi, Nisargadatta Maharaj was a living example of the highest non–dualistic Advaitic Truth. He is considered by some to be one of the most profound spiritual teachers of this age. Compiled from tapes of his talks and dialogues.

Peace Pilgrim's Wisdom
by Peace Pilgrim, edited by Cheryl Canfield (early 1995)

Peace Pilgrim was a genuine American saint who for 28 years lived on the road in faith, not accepting money or asking for food or shelter. She was a witness for inner and outer peace. Cheryl Canfield spent much time with her and helped compile and edit, along with four others, *Peace Pilgrim — Her Life and Work in Her Own Words*, currently with over 400,000 copies in print. This inspirational book has one of her sayings for each day of the year.

Sri Krishna Lila — The Life of a Divine Incarnation
by Devi Vanamali (November 1994)

The complete life of Krishna, from his remarkable birth to his death. This non-sectarian account of one believed by many in India to be a divine incarnation has powerful insights into applying the teachings of this many leveled story in our everyday lives. It is a tale lightly and charmingly told.

The Golden Treasury of Spiritual Wisdom
compiled by Andrew William (April 1995)

This book contains about 7,000 spiritually oriented sayings from sages, saints and ordinary people, providing cutting insights and uncommon wisdom, designed to help the reader with his or her struggle to lead a holy life.

To learn more about these and our other books write or call for our free newsletter, "The Blue Dove." Phone 1-800-691-1008 or write to our address given on last page of this book.

This book is the first in a trilogy by Swami Ramdas about his pilgrimage experience. The next two volumes, *In the Vision of God*, volumes I & II, are also published by Blue Dove Press. If your local bookstore does not carry them, you can obtain them directly from Blue Dove Press.

The name Blue Dove signifies peace and spirituality. Blue Dove Press publishes books by and about saints of all of the religions of the world as well as on other spiritually oriented topics. It also distributes books by other publishers on similar topics. To receive our free catalog or our free newsletter, "The Blue Dove," or our catalog of other books by Swami Ramdas, contact:

Blue Dove Press
Post Office Box 261611
San Diego, CA 92196
phone: 800-691-1008
FAX: 619-271-5695

To receive "Om Sri Ram," a free newsletter for people interested in the life, example and message of Swami Ramdas, write to:

The Satsang Foundation
P. O. Box 261243
San Diego, CA 92196